The King With
The Iron Belt

The King With
The Iron Belt

The life of
King James IV of Scotland

Jackie Cosh

Published by JC Publications

© Copyright Jackie Cosh 2018

THE KING WITH THE IRON BELT

All rights reserved.

ISBN 978-1-527-23805-3.

Book formatted by www.bookformatting.co.uk.

Contents

Jackie Cosh is a writer and journalist.

She can be contacted at

Jackiemcosh@yahoo.com

or via Twitter @ScotHistAuthor

Introduction

We all have someone in our lives who we have known for so long that we struggle to remember our first encounter. So it is with King James IV of Scotland. I remember discussing him in late 1998 while shopping for my wedding, but can't recall how I first became interested in him. I was desperate to read anything on my new interest that I could get my hands on, but I soon discovered that, unlike many other Scottish historical figures such as Mary Queen of Scots or William Wallace, there wasn't much in the way of books to choose from.

This saddened and bemused me. He was, after all, the man who married England's princess, Margaret Tudor, a marriage which led eventually to the joining of the two kingdoms. No other Scottish monarch, before or after him, did more for the Scottish navy than James IV, and the tale of his having worn an iron belt as penance for the part he played in his father's death is just one part of the chronicle that was the complicated Stewart family dynamics in the late sixteenth century.

Even if he had not been king and had perhaps just been an ordinary man living in rural Scotland, his life, and his unusual hobbies and interests, would have made him worthy of writing about. But what books I could find were academic in nature, aimed primarily at the history student studying this era. I can't fault the books in terms of their content, but I was looking for something a bit more reader friendly.

Over the course of the next 18 years I set out to read anything and everything I could find on James IV. I met up with others with a similar interest such as Elspeth Crocket, and even managed a visit to see the king's ring, sword and dagger at the College of Arms in London.

Along the way I gleaned as much information as I could, with the view to writing a book on King James IV aimed at the history reader, not the history scholar. Too few people know anything about this great man, and this book sets out to right that wrong.

Chapter 1

Father-Son Relations

On 17 March 1473 celebrations began in Scotland, for the queen had given birth to a baby boy, the new heir to the Scottish throne. Named James like his father, his grandfather and his great grandfather before him, King James IV of Scotland was the sixth Stewart king to rule Scotland. During his reign the Scottish navy would be built up to the strongest it had ever been, Scotland would take huge strides forward in the fields of education and law, and, through his marriage to Margaret Tudor of England, the two countries would eventually be united as one country.

James was the first child of King James III and his wife Margaret of Denmark. Margaret was the daughter of King Kristian I of Norway, Denmark and Sweden, and of his wife Dorothea of Brandenburg. She had been betrothed to James in 1460, at the age of four. For years Scotland and Denmark had fought over the issue of taxation of the Hebrides, and the French king had put forward the proposal of the marriage in order to end the feud.

Nine years later Margaret arrived in Scotland and the marriage ceremony took place in July 1469 in Holyrood Abbey in Edinburgh. Upon the marriage King Kristian's ambassador presented his new son-in-law with the Order of the Elephant, the Danish order of chivalry, and the highest order of Denmark.

The bride brought with her the promise of a dowry of 60,000 guilders, 10,000 of which was to be paid in cash, with the Orkney and Shetland Islands pledged as security. But by 1472 the dowry had still not been paid, so, after four years of negotiations the

Scottish Parliament passed an Act to make Orkney and Shetland part of Scotland. Legitimate male heirs of King Kristian I could in theory take them back by paying the dowry balance, but Scottish control of Orkney and Shetland by this time was so strong that the prospect was viewed as unlikely, and they have remained as part of Scotland ever since.

Edinburgh appears to have been the queen's home in the early years of her marriage and we know that she had a room and chapel in the royal apartments attached to Holyrood Abbey. From the information we have about James and Margaret they appear to have had a good marriage, in the early years at least, and Margaret was a good and loyal wife. They made a trip to the north-east of Scotland together and at least two trips to Falkland where they went hunting. Most importantly the queen produced children, and male children at that.

When we consider that many families, and even many royal families, at that time would have experienced the heartbreak of miscarriages, of stillbirths and of children dying during infancy, the fact that the royal couple were blessed with three children who all lived to adulthood is quite an achievement in itself.

The country would also have been relieved that the children were boys. When in the next century James V died, he left Scotland with a baby princess, resulting in years of turmoil for the country. And as Henry VII of England was to find out, often one son was not enough. When his eldest son Prince Arthur died as a young man, he was at least fortunate that he had a younger son, the future Henry VIII, to continue the dynasty.

The king was 21 at the time of the birth of their first son; his wife just 16. Unfortunately, few records survive from this time, so instead we have to put together the pieces of the jigsaw from what little information we do have.

The new prince was born during a time of relative peace in Scotland and the truce between Scotland and England was renewed when James was a week old. He was most likely born at Stirling Castle, for this was now the chief residence of his mother, the queen, and where he spent most of his childhood under the watch of his mother, and, latterly, James Shaw of Sauchie, Stirling Castle's keeper and the governor his father had appointed.

Created Duke of Rothesay at an early age (the traditional title given to the Scottish king's firstborn son) and Earl of Carrick, most historians agree that the queen played a big part in his upbringing and that his father, the king, was a distant figure in the child's life. He certainly appears to have built up a close relationship with his mother, whereas the relationship with his father seems to have been one built only on duty.

At the end of July of that year the king and queen went on a pilgrimage to St Ninian's Shrine at Whithorn in Galloway. St Ninian built Scotland's first recorded Christian church in Whithorn in the fifth century and many monarchs made pilgrimages to it.

Royal accounts tell us that six ladies in waiting went with her, all with new outfits, and that new baggage was bought for the trip. They may have been giving thanks for the safe birth of their first son who was to later make almost yearly trips to the shrine.

Rothesay was born into the Stewart dynasty which had begun a hundred years earlier when Robert Stewart took the throne to become King Robert II, and which was to continue for another three hundred years. His father James III had become king at the age of nine when his own father died. He took personal control in 1468 at the age of 17 but those years of his minority rule were to mar his whole reign and he was not a popular king.

In many ways James III turned out to be the kind of man who really shouldn't have been king. Whether that was because of his natural personality or because of manipulation by the Scottish lords it is hard to tell, although one is inclined to think that it was a combination of both.

During his minority his counsellors had done their best to keep hold of the reins of the country by dissuading him from studying the business of the country. Consequently, he grew up to be a man who was more interested in the arts and architecture than in the politics and business of running the country.

Described as a weak and incompetent ruler, James III was criticised for his lack of foreign policy. He was often manipulated by those who were supposed to support him, to the point that even the birth of his son and heir was clouded by their negative comments and advice.

One would assume that James would have been delighted at the birth of his first son. With an heir to the throne the continuation of the Stewart dynasty was safe and a male heir secured his position even further. What did he have to worry about?

But the astrologers spoke of the planets being in the wrong position and seeds of doubt were planted. When Bishop John Leslie wrote an account of the prince's birth, he wrote about an amazing comet which appeared in the south for a month before the birth, describing it as a sign of marvellous changes to the world. But Leslie was writing approximately a century later. Contemporary chroniclers took a different view, describing it as a sign of disasters to follow.

Prophecies were discovered or made up of how danger would come from within the family. Witches were brought to the king to tell him that his downfall would come from his next of kin. He did have two brothers, and of less importance, sisters, but suspicion must also have fallen on the new prince.

The king does not appear to have got to know his eldest son very well or to have visited him often. Events throughout his reign made him paranoid and there was always someone there to reinforce these fears. James III was not very good at choosing wise strong men to help run his country. If he did suspect his son of planning against him, keeping a distance between them must have seemed like a way of protecting himself from danger.

Suspicion does not appear to have fallen on Rothesay's younger brothers James and John. Perhaps James realised that if a rebellion was to happen it was most likely to come in the name of his eldest son as opposed to one of his two younger sons, who would have had to depose both the king and his heir in order to have benefited.

The fact that the king and queen named their second son James is also often cited as evidence that Rothesay was a sickly child and that they named the second son James in case the first one should die. This may have been the case; lack of records makes it impossible for us to know for sure, but it was not necessarily the reason. It was not unheard of for families to have two or more sons with the same first name. In addition, it must be remembered that kings sometimes chose to rule under a different name from their birth name, so it wasn't necessary for the future king to be named James at birth.

In February 1478 the queen was officially given custody and entrusted with the education of her eldest son, although this is likely to have been just a formality. All the signs were that she played a big part in his childhood and that of his brothers, and from what we can gather the three brothers were brought up with their mother at Stirling.

One area which she would have taken a back seat to and which King James took much interest in was the young prince's marriage potential. At the time of his birth Edward IV was king of England, and when the young Rothesay was a year old, he became betrothed to Cecilia, the three-year-old daughter of the English king.

In October 1474 English ambassadors arrived in Edinburgh, and at the Dominican Friary the Earl of Argyll, Master of the Household and James Shaw of Sauchie, the Earl of Crawford, took the marriage vows on behalf of the infant Rothesay, with the English Lord Scope replying for the three-year-old princess.

The actual marriage was to take place when both reached marriageable age, with the bride bringing a dowry of 20,000 marks sterling, to be paid in advance, in annual instalments of 2,000 marks. However, the marriage was never realised and this was in fact the first of three marriage treaties which the king was to organise for his son, none of which came to anything. The main aim of the marriage treaty was to bring peace to the two kingdoms, and it did result in a truce for a while.

But by 1483 Edward IV was dead and Richard III was on the throne. A marriage was proposed between Rothesay and Anne de la Pole, niece of the English king, as part of a peace agreement between the two countries. The marriage was to take place within three years of the truce. But within the year Richard III had been killed at the Battle of Bosworth.

For all his concern about Rothesay, James III was not naïve enough to forget that he also had two adult brothers who posed a threat. He was the first king since Robert III to have adult siblings. For kings and queens, having plenty of healthy children was their aim; after all there was always the risk that the heir to the throne might die or be killed. James II became king after his elder twin's death. His father James I was the youngest of three sons, both of whom died before he was eight. To secure the lineage it was important to have at least one back-up son – the heir and the spare so to speak.

But from the point of view of ruling kings, siblings, particularly adult male siblings, were a threat. Robert III had to contend with dealing with them. When the Scottish Parliament intervened and appointed the weak king's eldest son David, Duke of Rothesay, to govern for him, the king's brother, Albany, imprisoned his nephew, who died in mysterious circumstances in 1402.

Whether it was a self-fulfilling prophecy or not, James III's fears of his firstborn were to eventually come true. But first he had his siblings to contend with. Like his forefathers before him adult siblings were to prove to be a curse.

James III had two brothers who survived childhood – Alexander, Duke of Albany, and John, Earl of Mar. James's two brothers were said to have been jealous of him, hating him for the amount of time he spent with scholars.

Events kicked off in 1479 when both his brothers rebelled against him. Firstly, the king's youngest brother, John, Earl of Mar, was accused of witchcraft and of trying to kill the king and he was placed in confinement where he died. Various rumours spread about how he died, ranging from those which made the king seem like a hero to those which made him out to be a coldblooded murderer.

One tale has James killing his brother, and not surprisingly this one stuck until James's death. Another one has James removing his brother from Craigmillar Castle when he contracted a fever and taking him to the Canongate in Edinburgh where he was seen by his own physicians.

Several women were arrested, on the accusation of performing witchcraft and of conspiring with the earl against the king. They were brought to trial and killed.

The king made the royal favourite, Robert Cochrane, the new Earl of Mar. Nobody could get near the king because of him, further alienating him from the lords. James III was very fond of having favourites, not necessarily well chosen, and this was to lead to his downfall.

Around the same time his other brother, Alexander, Duke of Albany, began to cause him problems and he was also imprisoned for plotting against the king. Albany was kept in Edinburgh Castle where it was said that he invited his jailors to dinner and drank with them until they feel asleep. He then escaped through the window aided by his servant, and made his way to Dunbar, where he fled to France.

Albany was made welcome by King Louis XI when he arrived in France in the autumn of 1479 and there he married Anne de La Tour. But King Louis was not prepared to help him fight against his brother, the king, and so Albany eventually turned to England.

Landing at Southampton in April 1482 Albany was escorted to London to meet with King Edward, where he received a more promising welcome. Despite already being married, King Edward promised him his daughter Cecilia as a bride.

At Fotheringhay on 10 June he signed a treaty promising to do homage to King Edward six months after taking possession of the Scottish crown, to break the Auld Alliance with France, to abstain from any new alliance which would not please England, and to surrender Berwick to England two weeks after capturing Edinburgh. Edward promised to help 'Alexander, King of Scotland' gain possession of his kingdom.

Three years after he had left Scotland, and with the assistance of Richard, Duke of Gloucester, Albany gathered an English army and marched north to Berwick. One part of the treaty at least was fulfilled. Berwick was seized by the English and this was to be the last time the town changed hands.

Meanwhile James had gathered an army at Boroughmuir, near Edinburgh. They marched on to Lauder, where they were met by another army under the leadership of the earls of Angus, Huntly and Lennox. The Scottish currency had become debased, a fact that James appeared to be ignoring. The nobles asked him to recall the coinage and to give his favourites up for justice. If he did that they would march with him. The king refused and so the lords took action. Capturing James's men, all apart from the 18-year-old Sir John Ramsay (who clung so tightly to the king that they were afraid of hurting him if they took him by force) were taken to the bridge and hung.

With the king and his nobles at war, fighting Albany and the English was no longer deemed possible and the army was disbanded. The king was taken to Edinburgh Castle where he was held prisoner under the guardianship of his half-uncle John Stewart, Earl of Atholl and James Stewart, Earl of Buchan.

So, when Albany arrived in Edinburgh he was met with a different scene from what he had expected. His brother, the king, was in prison and the 'Lauder Lords' were now in charge.

Opinions were divided on Albany, but none of the lords fully trusted him and he knew it. Grasping what he must have viewed as his best option, he signed a peace treaty with the lords, whereby his previous titles and estates were restored on condition that he remain faithful to the king.

It has been suggested that in the days following the truce with the Lauder Lords, Albany assured King Edward that he was still loyal to him. Whether this was true or not, he appears to have been keeping his options open and his next move was to travel to Stirling Castle where the queen was living with the three young princes.

At Stirling he spent some time talking with the queen, discussing Rothesay's education. On her advice he then rode to Edinburgh Castle where he set the king free.

The fact that Albany placed so much importance in speaking to the queen shows that he was aware that she was more than simply a figurehead and that she did wield some power. The extent of her part in the rebellion is not certain but we do know that the breakdown in their marriage can be dated to this period, for from then on they were estranged.

Albany's heroic freeing of the king may well have just been for show, for it is likely that the queen was in contact with the Stewart half-uncles who were responsible for holding him prisoner. Certainly, her salaried keeper, John Stewart, Lord Darnley had access to the king when he was imprisoned in Edinburgh Castle, and the queen still had custody of Edinburgh Castle, which had been given to her earlier in her marriage.

A few days later the king made Albany his Lieutenant General in Scotland, Lord High Admiral and Warden of the East and West Marches and made him the new Earl of Mar.

For the next short while the brothers spent much of their time together, eating together and, as was the custom of the time, sharing a bed. But Albany was still colluding with the English and it was not long before King James found out about this and the closeness ended.

Retaliating, Albany accused the king of trying to poison him and withdrew to his castle in Dunbar. At this point the king showed some strength and called parliament. At this Albany backtracked, admitting that he had been lying when he had accused his brother of poison; denouncing any treaties he had made with England; resigning as Lieutenant General, and promising not to come within six miles of the king.

Early on in 1483 Albany again tried and failed to seize the king. He must have been losing hope, and when Edward IV died on 9 April 1483, he knew the picture was now quite different. He fled to England, letting an English garrison into Dunbar Castle as he left.

Still not giving up, Albany made one last attempt to invade Scotland in July 1484. Along with the exiled James, Earl of Douglas, and five hundred horsemen, he crossed the border on 22 July. The battle only lasted a matter of hours for Richard III was now king and he was keen to make peace with Scotland.

Albany fled to France one last time but did not live for long. He died in Paris from a wound sustained in a joust. His death meant that King James III now had no siblings left to rebel against him, only sons.

Chapter 2

The Road To Kingship

The crisis of 1482 had been dealt with and James III was still king. But it had changed the king and queen's relationship forever, and with Rothesay under the guardianship of his mother it would have had an impact on the relationship Rothesay had with his father.

By 1483 Rothesay was now ten years old, young by today's standards, but he was described by chroniclers as a mature boy for his age, advanced for his years. While it is important to remember that chroniclers did tend to be complimentary to the kings they wrote about, Rothesay's actions on becoming king and on taking power (at the relatively young age of 15) certainly substantiate these claims. However, it cannot have helped the father-son relationship that his father appears to have kept him away from taking any part in the government, even as a bystander, ignoring the fact that he was slowly reaching adulthood.

From the time of the 1482 rebellion to the time of Sauchieburn, Rothesay rarely saw his father, if at all. These years are the ones where most fathers tend to become closer to their sons as they reach the age where they can relate to them more.

Rothesay disappears from the records from late 1482 to the start of 1488 and he doesn't appear to have made any trips to Edinburgh to see his father, certainly none were recorded. Relationships between his mother and father were now frosty and would remain so until her death. Rightly or wrongly the king blamed his wife for what he felt was the part she played in the rebellion, believing that she had colluded with Albany from the start and that the siege of

Stirling Castle had all been for show.

For a king such as James III this should also have been the age where he began showing his son the ropes, introducing him to aspects of government and to running the country, in many ways beginning an apprenticeship which in reality could end at any time.

One would also think that if James believed the witches' prophecies that danger would come from his nearest kin, that the most sensible action to take would be to get to know his son, and to build up a close bond with him. Instead James III took a very different course of action, doing everything he could to alienate his eldest son.

However, he appears to have been happy to leave Rothesay in the care of his mother. He could easily have removed the boy from her as a form of punishment, but while he built up resentment against his wife, he didn't show this by being openly vengeful to her.

King James's interest in his son was in the part he could play in international relations. At Nottingham in September 1484 a marriage treaty was drawn up between Rothesay and Anne de la Pole, niece of King Richard III. The marriage was to take place within three years; however, less than 11 months later Richard III was killed at the Battle of Bosworth. With the Tudor Henry VII now in power the marriage treaty was now obsolete.

At this point James's actions become more interesting, perhaps hinting at a growing gulf between him and Rothesay. In July 1486 the king signed another three-year truce with England, which included a marriage alliance between his second son, James, Marquis of Ormonde, and Katharine, the fourth surviving daughter of Edward IV.

Rothesay was now 13, moving rapidly towards adulthood, and his father was now beginning to show his resentment towards his eldest son. He and his mother must have viewed this as a public insult.

Neither did the relationship between Rothesay and the king improve when Queen Margaret died on 14 July 1486. The queen was only 30 years old, so still a young woman. The rumour soon spread that the king had poisoned the queen, and when Rothesay defeated his father two years later, he was to use this tale to justify his actions to the Danes. While it was unlikely that there was any truth in this story, it does tell us something about how both were viewed by the Scottish people.

The fact that they had been living apart for some time had not gone unnoticed and perhaps the king made his anger with the queen known in ways which have not been recorded. But what does seem apparent is that the rift between the two was well established and common knowledge.

In another story surrounding her death the queen is also painted as innocent and virtuous. When her biographer Giovanni Sabadino wrote an account of her death, he told of her calling Rothesay to her deathbed, and of her pleading for him to live a good and godly life, warning him against using violence.

Again, this may well be a story which was devised to fit in to subsequent events and which would have sat well alongside the story of the queen being poisoned. It was convenient to tell a story where the queen appears to foretell the events of 1488 when violence would kill her husband and put her son on the throne.

Whether it was true or not, the king was now free to remarry, not for love, but for international relations. Eighteen months after the death of his wife, James signed a marriage treaty with England which incorporated the earlier treaty from the year before. But as well as the Ormonde marriage, he proposed a marriage with himself and Elizabeth Woodville, the widow of Edward IV. Rothesay was remembered in the treaty, but the proposal was for him to marry one of Edward IV's other daughters. He does appear to have been an afterthought.

The king does not seem to have learned anything from the rebellion of 1482. His resentment towards his eldest son, and the anger which he had built up towards his wife, were the two lasting effects of the revolt. A change in policy, better judgement of advisors and of the political climate, were not.

While James put his time and energies into arranging marriages for him and his son, he would really have been better off spending his time sorting out his home affairs. The majority of the Scottish lords were not supportive of him and he only made matters worse by alienating powerful families.

One example was the Humes, and the king's feud with them came to a head in 1487. The Humes had, for the past 14 years, been opposing James's plans to make Coldingham Priory into a Collegiate College to help fund the Chapel Royal.

Coldingham Priory in Berwickshire dated back to the reign of David I and was an old Benedictine monastery which had become very wealthy. Pope Innocent VIII had recently made John Hume prior of Coldingham, but still the king made the threat that anyone who opposed his plans would be charged with treason.

By the end of January 1488, he had called a committee of 50, almost two thirds of the parliament, to take action against those who had broken the Coldingham statute.

Top of this list was of course John Hume, and the king threatened the Hume family, their friends and relatives, with charges of treason. Unfortunately for James the Humes had plenty of friends and one by one they began to show their allegiances. These friends included James Shaw of Sauchie, Rothesay's keeper at Stirling Castle. He had recently married his daughter Helen off to Patrick Hume.

The mounting dissatisfaction with the king was not confined to the dispute over Coldingham. There was growing unrest around the country and James was becoming more aware of this. Keen to gather support, in January 1488 he extended royal control over the administration of justice. This was in contrast to the legislation he had passed in the previous October where civil cases were to be referred to their judges ordinary. By improving the running of the criminal system, which he had taken little to do with throughout his reign, he hoped to impress potential allies.

But instead of going out to these areas himself, he appointed justiciars to do the work for him. His actions did not impress anyone and his indecision, by overturning the October legislation, made him look inconsistent. If he thought he would make friends by taking an interest in the justice system then he was a few years too late.

On 29 January, the last day of the parliament, James rewarded those who had supported him in the past and made peace with others. Crichton of Sanquhar, Drummond of Cargill, Hay of Yester, and Ruthven of Yester became new lords of parliament. David Kennedy, William Carlyle and Robert Cunningham of Polmaise became knights.

If the king was looking to increase the number of royal supporters, this was cancelled out when he created one more title. His second son, James, Marquis of Ormonde, Earl of Ross and Lord of Brechin was made Duke of Ross and Earl of Edirdale. Yet again the king snubbed his eldest son.

Word quickly got to Stirling and on 2 February Rothesay, along with James Shaw of Sauchie, left Stirling without his father's knowledge or consent. Contemporary accounts are lacking as to his reasons for taking this course of action, and we must be reliant on chroniclers from the following century to gain some idea of where he may have gone and how his actions were justified.

Piecing together the different accounts, it looks likely that he was moved to Linlithgow and that the rebels issued a declaration to explain why they had removed him without his permission. To gain public support they would have had to have made the king look bad, justifying their actions by giving the story that they were protecting Rothesay.

It may have been around this time that rumours began to circulate that James III had poisoned the queen. And the rebels may have used the excuse that they were trying to protect Rothesay from his father. It is unknown to what extent the rebels had to go to in order to persuade Rothesay to join them or what his initial feelings were.

Meanwhile matters were not going any better for the king. For reasons unknown he dismissed his chancellor, Colin Campbell, Earl of Argyll, one of his most active and loyal servants. He appears to have started to panic and to lose his judgement in the way people often do when they don't know which way to turn. He knew he was in trouble and was scrambling about trying to find out who was friend and who was foe.

On 21 February he disbanded the committee of 50 which had been set up to deal with the perceived treason from the Coldingham saga. In March he made a significant step when he left Edinburgh, heading north towards Aberdeen. The rebels were nearby in Linlithgow and the fact that he left Edinburgh shows that he was feeling threatened.

The king left the city, but not before he sent George Robison, the comptroller, ahead with 1,000 pounds of royal funds. The money was to be used to buy James favour.

At the same time, John Ramsay, who had now been made Lord Bothwell, was sent to England to ask for help from King Henry VII.

Even with a large sum of money to buy support, James did not do well in Aberdeen. He had been advised to negotiate with the rebels. This he did by signing a list of subjects to be discussed by both sides, but he then reneged on this when he left Aberdeen to settle the situation by force. Unfortunately for him, most of the lords who at first appeared to be supporting him refused to join him. Their desired course of action was to negotiate and talk, rather than fight.

He did, however, succeed in gaining, or perhaps buying, the support of his three half-uncles – Andrew Stewart, Bishop of Moray, John Stewart, Earl of Atholl and James, Earl of Buchanan. To the Bishop of Moray he bestowed the cathedral church of Moray, as well as the barony and burgh of Spynie in free regality. Atholl received funds from the king, probably to enable him to raise troops for the king.

It is interesting to note at this point that James turned to his three half-uncles who had previously held him prisoner during the crisis of 1482.

After leaving Aberdeen the king headed for Blackness Castle, where he was met for the first time by the rebels. A small fight broke out and the king was forced into agreeing to negotiate. Four hostages were taken by the rebels, to ensure that he kept his word, but he didn't and by May he was back at Edinburgh Castle.

Scant details survive of Rothesay's activities during this time, but we do know that in May he appointed commissioners to negotiate with the Master of Crawford and others. He does not, however, appear to have made attempts to be reconciled with his father. Instead he treated him very much as the enemy and was calling himself Prince of Scotland.

In early June the king left Edinburgh for the last time and headed for Stirling. He did have some genuine supporters, but many were there because they had been bought.

Events kicked off with the royalists burning Sir William of Keir's estate, a supporter of the rebels, who was later knighted by Rothesay when he became King James IV. Rothesay then left Stirling Castle with a rebel force where he was met by the royalist John Ross of Montgrenan who chased him south.

On Thursday 11 June 1488, between the Sauchie and Bannock burns, both sides met to fight the battle which through time would become known as the Battle of Sauchieburn. It was said that Rothesay had ordered that nobody was to lay a finger on his father.

The king had met David, second Lord Lindsay, in Fife, where he had given the king his horse as a gift. Afterwards this was to be viewed as ominous.

We have little information on the battle itself, maybe because the real action of that day did not happen on the battlefield itself but nearby. Pursued by the fierce Borderers the king escaped towards Stirling on his own.

The story of what happened next has been embellished throughout the years and one must accept that a bit of drama was added to the story to spice it up. We shall look at the dramatised, detailed version first.

The king, it was said, rode through the Bannock burn and on crossing the burn he startled a woman who was carrying water to the nearby mill. Alarmed, probably from the speed of the rider than of anything else, she dropped her pitcher and ran away. This sound scared the king's horse, who leapt over the stream and stopped suddenly, throwing James to the ground.

Not knowing who he was, the miller and his wife took him to

their house where he asked for a priest. When they asked who he was he said: 'This day at morn I was your king'.

The miller's wife ran to find a priest and brought back a man named Borthwick who happened to be passing.

'Here I am, I am a priest,' he said. 'Where is the king?'

Borthwick, it was said, recognised the king and kneeling down beside him asked him if he thought he would survive if he received treatment. The king replied that he thought he would, but that he needed a priest to give him the sacrament.

'That shall I do hastily,' said Borthwick, taking out a dagger which he used to strike him in the heart and kill him.

This is the story which is often told about James III's death – a dramatic end to a disastrous reign. But how much of it is true?

It is more than likely that only some of this story is true. Another version has the king being pursued and killed at Bannockburn Mill. Contemporary records do not name his killer and it is not until the sixteenth century that a suggestion that he was killed by a servant of Lord Gray was put forward.

Certainly, in the aftermath, with his son James IV now on the throne, there appears to be no mention of the late king's killer or who he was and records state that he was slain by an unnamed man after fleeing the battlefield.

We also do not know who found the king's body or when it was found. Most likely it was found pretty soon after. But Rothesay wasted no time in declaring himself king. On 12 June, one day after the battle, and most likely just a few hours after his father's death, he issued his first charter as King James IV of Scotland. The witches' predictions had unfortunately come true, and the reign of King James IV had begun.

Chapter 3

The New King

So, at 15 the young James was now king of Scotland. Both his parents were dead, and his brothers were too young to provide any kind of support. It is unlikely that when he agreed to join the rebel forces he had foreseen or even considered the reality of his actions and of his becoming king so soon. But this was now the reality.

Two weeks after the battle he was crowned king at Scone. Although this had become the traditional place for Scottish kings to be crowned, neither his father nor his grandfather had been crowned there; the first having been crowned at Kelso Abbey, with his grandfather crowned at Holyrood Abbey in Edinburgh. The late king, meanwhile, was to be buried at Cambuskenneth Abbey, not far from his queen.

James was like many 15-year-old princes of the time. He was full of life, enjoyed hunting and hawking, as well as entertainment such as music and dancing. At first he showed no interest in more serious pursuits and it looked as if he was going to be a puppet king, for the first few years at least. He wouldn't have been the first puppet king to have been played by the lords and he wouldn't be the last. But he was soon to prove to be quite a different king from what they had predicted, and perhaps hoped.

The new king, it was said, was overcome with grief at what he had done and the part he had played, and interestingly it was to Stirling, his father's favourite castle, that he headed for once he was crowned. There he spent time coming to terms with events and he sought counsel with the priest from the chapel there about how to be free of his guilt.

At Stirling he was said to be 'sad and dolorous' so entertainment was provided to cheer him up and to take his mind off the situation. There was dancing, plays performed and hunting parties. It couldn't be said that he had had a close relationship with his father, but he had still played a part in engineering the downfall of a royal prince and felt some remorse.

As well as horrifying neighbouring royal families, who would have been aware that if this had happened in Scotland it could happen anywhere, it had caused unrest at home, so there was only so much time he could spend grieving. It was imperative that he take full control of the kingdom as soon as possible and that he take action to prove that the fighting and his father's death had not been in vain. There were two problems – how to prove to the country that the winning side were worthy of running the country, and were not simply rebels, but also how to deal with the losing side. Should they be punished?

The king wasted no time in taking charge. On 7 July he presided over a meeting of the Lords of the Exchequer. On 12 July the Lords of Council got back to business again. Before the end of August he was in Lanark presiding over the justice ayre, and in the evenings being entertained by dancers and guisers. He was making his presence known.

In September the king travelled to Dunfermline with his hawks and falconers, and from there he went to Dundee where he presided over the justice ayre, made Lord Hailes Great Admiral of Scotland, and bought horses for his falcons. For all the initial concerns that he would be a puppet king, he was quick enough in proving himself otherwise.

He was also not slow in dealing with his father's supporters. Of course, this could not be avoided. And it certainly looks like he took on the task because it had to be done, rather than from any bad feeling, or need for revenge.

Only ten of the late king's supporters were summoned to stand trial for treason, and the charges against all but four (Buchan, Bothwell, Ross of Montgrenan and Murray of Cockpule) were quietly dropped before Parliament met.

Elphinstone, the man who had supported the late king until the end, was deprived of the position of chancellor. However, when he appeared in Parliament at the start of October he was chosen to be one of the Lords Auditors of Causes and Complaints, and by the end of the month he was on the bench with the Lords of Council.

The first Parliament of the new reign opened in Edinburgh on Monday 6 October 1488, with 34 bishops, abbots, clerics of lower degree; ten earls; and 25 lords and commissioners from 16 burghs. The king did not appear on the first day. This was not unusual. Standard practice was for the king to appoint certain nobles to act on his behalf – in this case Argyll, Hailes, Lyle and Hume.

The king attended on the second day and the Lords Auditors of Causes and Complaints and the Lords of the Articles were elected. To the first committee (comprised of three clerics including Elphinstone, two nobles and three burgesses) Parliament delegated it powers of a civil court. To the second (consisting of nine clerics, 14 nobles and five burgesses) it entrusted the drafting of new legislation.

A group of six nobles was appointed to sit in judgement on Buchan and his allies the following day. Meanwhile members who had not been elected to a committee were free to do their own thing. None of the accused appeared on the day appointed. On 9 October Buchan appeared, and pled guilty to the charges of engaging in treasonable negotiations with England and to encouraging the late king in breaking his first agreement with his nobles. Apologising to the king, he received an unconditional pardon.

Bothwell and Ross of Montgrenan, who were not present, but had escaped to England, were found guilty of treason and sentenced to lose life, land and goods. The case against the Laird of Cockpule was postponed for another three months.

On 17 October the Parliament reassembled for its final meeting. Having punished the late king's supporters, it was now time to give rewards to the winning side. Lord Hailes was given Bothwell's estates, including his castles at Bothwell and Crichton, as well as his title; Hume, Laird of Fastcastle in the Borders was given the lands of Montgrenan. Royal officials from both sides were suspended from office for three years. Merchants and other men of substance who had supported James III were refused compensation. But the heirs of those who had fallen were to be allowed to succeed to their estates.

The victors did appear to be acting pretty leniently, perhaps because they felt that they were on trial themselves. They persuaded Parliament to declare that the agreement they had had with the late king had been broken and so the new king and his supporters were innocent of any wrongdoing. This is more evidence that they felt they needed to prove themselves to neighbouring countries and rulers, for copies of this proclamation were sent to the pope and the kings of France, of Spain and of Denmark. Ambassadors were also sent to the continent to 'see and consider' a suitable bride for the king, from the princesses of Europe, but also to renew the Auld Alliance with France.

The Auld Alliance dated back to 1295 when John Balliol and Philip IV of France signed the treaty against Edward I of England. The treaty stated that should one of the countries be attacked by England, the other country would attack it also, so that England would be fighting a war on two fronts as opposed to one.

Emergency measures were put in place to deal with criminals throughout the country. Dividing Scotland into districts, a powerful noble (in most cases one of the victors of Sauchieburn) was given a district to police, with punishments being handed out either locally or by the king. This was to be the arrangement until the king came of age. From now on the king would attend all justice ayres, accompanied by the justiciar.

Parliament then adjourned until 14 January 1489, apart from the lord auditors who sat for a further nine days.

For all the initial reservations about the king turning out to be a puppet king, whose main focus was on enjoying himself and spending from the royal purse, he wasted no time in proving himself otherwise. Reports have him sitting with the Lords of Council, riding with the justice ayres at Selkirk and Peebles, and travelling to St Andrews, before stopping at Linlithgow for Christmas.

Business continued in January when Parliament decreed Glasgow should be made an archbishopric city. For Glasgow this was good news as it brought wealth and status to the town, and it went on to become one of the largest and wealthiest archbishoprics in Scotland. But it was to take some time for Rome to acknowledge this change in status.

The chancellor wrote to the pope informing him but received no reply. Then the king wrote several times. Again, there was silence. In 1490 he sent his clerk, Andrew Forman, to Rome, but there was no response from Pope Innocent.

Another letter followed from James, in which he voiced his frustration that his letters and requests had been ignored.

It wasn't until 9 January 1492 that the pope issued a papal bull separating the dioceses of Glasgow, Dunkeld, Dunblane, Galloway and Lismore from the province of St Andrews, making Glasgow a metropolitan church with jurisdiction over the other four dioceses.

Why the delay? It may well have been that Rome was busy. However, even when confirmation did come from Rome, there continued to be disputes over details and what privileges the new archbishop, Robert Blackader, was to have.

No doubt neither the king nor the rebels were naïve enough to think that all would be plain sailing in the new regime. And the ripples were not long in coming. On 8 January 1489 the Master of Huntly had written to King Henry in England, asking for his support for the friends and kinsmen of the late king, who were planning on banding together to avenge his death. He made clear that he intended to launch an attack on the new regime.

The English king, while tempted, had enough to contend with at that time and nothing came of this. This would also have been against the terms of the peace treaty between the two countries, signed in October 1488, where both sides had agreed a three-year truce. In addition, he had exchanged gifts with James in 1489.

Around this time Lord Forbes rode through Aberdeen and nearby towns, displaying the late king's torn and bloodstained shirt at the end of a long spear, and calling for his countrymen to avenge his death.

In March 1489, having presided over the justice ayres in the south-west, the king returned to Edinburgh to find that the justiciar had formed a treasonable alliance with the Earl of Lennox and his son Lord Matthew Stewart. While Lennox had been rewarded the previous year, he had felt that he had not been priority and had been made to wait longer than he believed he should have.

Others such as Robert, Lord Lyle, had begun to feel excluded from the new regime. There was growing feelings that some people were being favoured more than others, and as well as this the government was still continuing to take land from the rebels.

The government had been quick in dealing with matters at the beginning, but the situation was dragging on and was causing unrest. On 26 June 1489 the third parliament in nine months was called, in order to deal with the situation. In their absence Lennox and Lyle were found guilty of treason and sentenced to lose life, land and goods. A price of 1,000 marks was put on their heads, and it was arranged for the king to march against Lennox's castle at Crookston and Lyle's castle at Duchal, as well as Dumbarton Castle.

On 18 July the king left Linlithgow for Glasgow with his siege train, including the great cannon Mons Meg. Duchal Castle surrendered by the end of the month. But Dumbarton was not so easy and they were driven out when the rebels set fire to the town.

It was not until mid-December that the rebels were caught, so much of 1489 was taken up with trying to bring peace to the kingdom again. This, not surprisingly, ran into 1490 when, at the parliament of February 1490, Lennox put forward the argument that the sentences passed the previous June had not been legal as the summons had not mentioned the precise hour at which he had to stand trial. This was accepted. The decree annulled the sentence and their estates were restored to them.

Also, at this parliament the secret council was chosen, and the king was persuaded to submit to being guided completely by the secret council and to make no grants of lands or goods, safe conducts, respites or remissions without its consent. Every document signed by him was to be countersigned by the chancellor and by all other members of the council who were present.

Next on the agenda was dealing with crime and quashing any further signs of rebellion before they had the chance to turn into something serious. Bringing back a series of statutes from more than 60 years ago, designed to secure the swift arrest and punishment of those guilty of murder or maiming, it ordained that justice ayres should be held twice a year in spring and autumn and that the king's 'most noble person' was to preside when it was appropriate.

Why the focus on crime and punishment? The reason is more to do with the fact that James III had been a touch lackadaisical in his attitude to justice, than because of any significant problem with crime. Whether he purposely set out to be different from his father or not, this was just one of many ways in which he improved on the previous reign.

Another admirable change was the introduction of the law which forbade the immediate eviction of the tenant when an estate changed hands. From now on the new landlord had to let them stay until the next Whitsuntide.

Other new laws included a ban on football, golf, and other 'unprofitable sportes'. Some historians believe this was a move to reduce English influence on the country and prevent English sports and cultures slipping in.

Eighteen months on from the legislation relating to the matrimonial tax and a large part of it had still not been paid. The king had excused some from paying it and they were now told by Parliament that the letters of discharge they had received were no longer valid. Sheriffs, provosts and bailies who had defaulted in payment were also warned to pay up.

Once this was done Parliament sanctioned the payment of five thousand pounds to be made for a group, including the Earl of Bothwell, the Bishop of Blackader, the Dean of Glasgow and others to go to France, Spain and other countries they saw fit, in order to find the king a bride. Ambassadors were also to renew the old treaties of alliance with France.

Bothwell left for France in July, returning on 29 November with a treaty signed by the French Charles VIII. Sir James Ogilvie sailed for Denmark in May and a treaty of peace and alliance was signed between Scotland and Denmark, with King James confirming the treaty on Ogilvie's return.

At the Parliament in February 1492 the ambassadors were thanked for their time and effort. But as they were still no further forward with finding a bride another trip was ordered. This of course required more money, and so a second matrimonial tax of 1,000 pounds was ordered.

Meanwhile the truce with England was, like many truces, not going to plan. Shortly after Sauchieburn some of the late king's men had sought sanctuary in England, and Henry was providing one of them at least, the ex Lord Bothwell, now known as Ramsay of Balmain, with a pension of 100 marks a year.

Henry also overlooked breaches of the treaty at sea. In the summer of 1489 five heavily armed English ships attacked and plundered Scottish merchant ships in the Firth of Forth. They were only saved by Sir Andrew Wood attacking the English ships and forcing them to surrender at Dunbar.

This was one of many examples of Henry troublemaking. If he did not provide encouragement (highly unlikely) he certainly was very good at turning a blind eye.

He also caused much trouble on land. In April 1491 he lent £266.13.4 to James's great-uncle, the Earl of Buchan, and Sir Thomas Tod, his Master of the Mint, on condition that they delivered to him either James himself or his younger brother, James, Duke of Ross.

In October of that year the English Parliament, blaming the Scots for breaking the truce, decided that all Scots without official residency should be banished from England, to leave within 40 days. When it came to ratifying another truce between the two countries, instead of making the time span five years, as had been agreed at Coldstream, James made it eight months.

For a time it looked like war would be inevitable, and tensions had been rising. Certainly, the fact that the truce was for such a short time frame was not a good sign. But Henry had too many other issues on his plate. With a man at the French court claiming to be the son of the late Edward IV, and Henry's involvement in the Brittany–France dispute, he clearly did not want to divide his attention.

James too was not keen on war. Events in Inverness and in the islands required his attention as trouble was brewing there.

After 1490 the Parliament stopped nominating members to the secret council. The king now chose his own council and decided when and when not to follow its advice. As one Spanish visitor to court noted, 'He decides nothing without his council, but in great matters he acts according to his own judgement'.

Many people in Scotland still felt that the late king's murder had not been avenged, so in the February 1492 Parliament rewards of land were offered to anyone who could provide the names of those who had hurt the king, in order for these people to be punished.

Gradually many who were against the new king came round to liking and respecting him. His remorse for the part he played in his father's death was evident, and on the advice of his confessor he wore an iron belt around his waist as penance. Some reports say that additional links were added every three years.

He vowed to never accept absolution for his part in his father's death, even if it came from the pope himself, and to wear the iron belt for the rest of his life.

It had not been the easiest of transition periods. But nobody had expected it to be. The rebellion of 1489, on a scale similar to that of 1488, had been quashed effectively. The problem of how the two sides could move forward had been dealt with as effectively as possible, and even those who had been against the new king initially, had to agree that he was proving himself.

Those who expected, and also those who hoped, that he would be a puppet king, were to be disappointed.

Chapter 4

An Active King

By 1496 James was now a mature man of 23. He was increasingly leading the government himself, and this was the end of parliament being called on a regular basis. Instead the king increasingly relied on the royal council and no parliament was called between June 1496 and 11 March 1504.

From his father (and from his grandfather also) James had inherited the problem of the Highlands and Islands. Scotland, while one country, was very much a divided country. The Central Belt, just as it is today, was the more populated part of the country and was where the king spent much of his time and where his main castles were. Then there was the Highlands and Islands, viewed by many people as being where the savages lived.

Historically the Highlands had been ruled by the Lord of the Isles, a title first given to John of Islay as a reward for his family's assistance to Robert the Bruce at the Battle of Bannockburn in 1314. They had always considered themselves quite separate from their southern countrymen, to such an extent that in 1462 the Lord of the Isles made a treaty with Edward IV of England to conquer Scotland with him and the Earl of Douglas. The lordship specified the feudal duties of his subjects and was responsible for retaining law and order in that part of the country.

To the uninitiated today this may seem like the king was relinquishing control of part of his country, but it was a system that had worked for centuries and it meant that the king did not have to spend all his time trying to tame what most considered an unruly and wild people.

But increasingly this was not working. Notwithstanding the fact that the Lord of the Isles had a history of siding with the English against the Scottish king, there had been one too many incidences of the Lord of the Isles failing to control his subjects. In 1491 Alexander of Lochalsh, nephew of the Lord of the Isles and his assumed successor, invaded Ross, destroying the castle and town of Inverness. The Mackenzies drove them out but were no kinder in their looting than the original invaders had been.

In 1493 the minority government had made the decision to forfeit the lordship and in August of that year the king sailed for the Western Isles – the first king to have gone there since Robert the Bruce.

The island chiefs went to Dunstaffnage Castle, near Oban, to submit to the king, with the Lord of the Isles, John Macdonald, surrendering the following year. James maintained him as a member of the Royal Household, providing him with a pension of 200 marks, and, after two years allowed him to retire to Paisley Abbey where he died four years later.

James granted fresh charters of land (previously held by the Lord of the Isles) to the chiefs who had surrendered, and knighted Alexander of Lochalsh and John of Islay. But he still had to return to the Highlands twice in 1494. The second visit happened after John of Islay stormed the castle at Dunaverty and hanged the governor over the walls. He was soon captured and was taken to Edinburgh and killed.

After that the king controlled the Highlands and Islands through his agents – mostly Campbells and Gordons. But the Act of Revocation, recalling the powers of the Lord of the Isles, in March 1498, caused more trouble, and for a time the Islands still acted as a thorn in James's side. But in time the situation did settle down. Today the Lord of the Isles is a title held by the eldest son of the ruling British monarch, a nominal title only.

James certainly wasn't averse to instigating a bit of trouble of his own, particularly when it came to causing the English monarch grief. The ideal situation came about in the form of an English man called Perkin Warbeck.

Warbeck first appeared at the court of Burgundy around 1490, citing a claim to the English throne. At the time Henry Tudor was king of England, having defeated Richard III at the Battle of Bosworth Field in 1485. Richard's nephews, the uncrowned Edward V and his younger brother Richard of Shrewsbury, Duke of York, the so-called 'Princes in the Tower', had gone missing circa 1483, with their bodies never found.

For Henry VII, too early in his reign to feel secure, a claim from the house of York would have caused him to worry, particularly since the boy's identity had been confirmed by Margaret of York, sister of Edward IV, and the aunt of the princes.

Warbeck's story was that his brother had been murdered but that he had been spared due to his innocence. He claimed that he had been made to swear an oath not to reveal his identity for a certain number of years, and that he had lived on the continent for seven years under the protection of Yorkist loyalists, until his guardian returned to England, allowing him the freedom to make himself known.

He was certainly good at public relations and King James was not the only king he had been in touch with. Charles VIII of France received him, causing much irritation to Henry Tudor. He was expelled in 1492, under the terms of the Treaty of Etoples, in which Charles agreed not to shelter rebels and those planning against Henry VII.

Philip of Habsburg also welcomed him to his court. Henry complained and was ignored, resulting in a trade embargo on Burgundy.

By 1495 he had set his sights on England, and on 3 July 1495, funded by Margaret of Burgundy, he landed in Kent. But before he had a chance to disembark, 150 of his troops were chased back to the boat by the locals. Ireland did not prove any more fruitful, so he headed for Scotland in November where James prepared to welcome him as the prince he claimed to be. James moved to Stirling from Edinburgh and on 20 November James received

Warbeck. Afterwards he called a meeting of the Great Council to discuss Warbeck and his claim on the English throne. Many of the council members had their doubts about him but were quite happy to go to war with England over the matter.

Within weeks of his arrival the king had arranged Warbeck's marriage to his kinsman, the Lady Katherine Gordon, an outward sign that he believed Warbeck to be who he claimed to be. But, in reality, this was probably more for show than for anything else. If he had truly believed that this man had a claim on the English crown, he would have made a more highly esteemed marriage for him than the one he did.

James arranged a tournament to celebrate the marriage and provided Warbeck with a pension of £1,344 a year. But despite this, and his apparent belief in Warbeck, he was not initially keen on invading England on his behalf. When he did, it was with less enthusiasm than one would have expected, and matters were not helped by Perkin Warbeck's attitude.

In September 1496 James began his attack on England, beginning with the raid of Ellem in Berwickshire, and with his troops he spent that winter moving between border castles. Later, when they did eventually move into England, they did not get far before Perkin Warbeck announced that he had had enough. This would not have helped James's increasingly cool attitude to him. Yes, it was fun knowing that his support for Warbeck was irritating the English king, but even this satisfaction had a limited time span.

Then the situation changed thanks to events in the south of England. In the summer of 1497, having had enough of the heavy taxes imposed on them, a group of Cornishmen rose in rebellion and marched to London. This had an impact on the war with Scotland as soldiers had to be recalled from the north in order to defend London. It also impinged on finances, and to save on money, and also lives, Henry chose to pull out of the war with James, on certain conditions, one being that he hand over Perkin Warbeck. He also demanded that James send three of his men as ambassadors – Angus, Hume and the Bishop of Moray – to England. If James refused to hand over Perkin the ambassadors were to be sent to England, James was to travel to London for a personal interview with Henry and hostages should be taken.

Richard Fox, Bishop of Durham, was to be the negotiator and was given instructions that, should James try to negotiate, he was to accept whatever was offered. The English king was keen to avoid full-on war.

James, however, was not. He took Mons Meg and other large guns from Edinburgh Castle and fired them at Fox's castle at Norham. A week into the siege news came that the Earl of Surrey was only two days away with an army of 20,000 men. Upon hearing this, James abandoned the siege and headed back to Edinburgh, where he learned that Surrey's army was by this time attacking castles in the Berwick area.

The plan was for James to meet Surrey in Berwick. He went part of the way and then turned back. Why did he do this? Was this him changing his mind or was it that he felt he didn't stand a chance?

Neither is the answer. James was employing a centuries' old tactic of encouraging the English onto Scottish land to fight with the hope that the Scottish weather would do half their work for them.

It worked and after five days the English army withdrew from Scotland, with many of its men sick and dying. Surrey tried to persuade them to stay; he tried threatening them and he tried bribery in the form of advance payments, but nothing could make them stay in Scotland. James's clever tactic had won.

The Spanish diplomat, Pedro de Ayala then travelled to the English court to act as an ambassador for James. He was instructed to negotiate a new truce, to run until one year after the death of the survivor of the two kings. By 1498 both had ratified it and Isabella and Ferdinand of Spain had been chosen as arbitrators in any future disputes.

James meanwhile was left with the problem of what to do with his guest and in October he spent £200 shipping Warbeck's people out of the country. The following summer he did the same for Warbeck, and in July he sailed out of Ayr. In September he landed in Cornwall and he was captured a few weeks later in Hampshire.

From there he was taken to the Tower of London but was

released when he confessed to being an imposter. He and his wife were allowed to attend Henry's court for a time. However, when he tried to escape, he was captured and ended his life at the gallows at Tyburn.

For some of those on the losing side at Sauchieburn in 1488 the memories were still pretty raw, and while James had tried to smooth things over between the opposing sides, he had had limited success. Henry took advantage of what he would have seen as a weakness and used these men to gain information on the Scottish king, which he could use to his advantage.

Two of the most prominent, John Ramsay (previously Lord Bothwell until he lost his title) and James Stewart, Earl of Buchan, had in fact been receiving a pension of 100 marks a year from Henry since 1489. These men had also, in 1491, been involved in a plot to kidnap James IV and his younger brother James, Duke of Ross and hand them over to Henry Tudor. James does not appear to have been aware of this fact, nor the fact that they had been involved in an unsuccessful attempt to assassinate Perkin Warbeck, and Buchan was occasionally a member of the royal judicial council on sessions, something James would surely not have allowed if he had known what Buchan was planning.

Like his English counterpart, James also had to rely heavily on taxes from his people and in the first ten years of his reign taxation had become almost annual, needed for wars with England and in order to deal with the rebellions in the Highlands and Islands. It is not surprising that the people were starting to resent this, particularly when some of it was going towards helping other countries. A tax in 1501 was set to fund Blackader, Bothwell and Forman travelling to England in order to organise a marriage treaty. The 1502 tax, where James had to raise £12,000, was needed to pay for ships and men to go to Denmark to help his Uncle John deal with the Norwegian and Swedish subjects who were rebelling. This inevitably led to arrears.

James had to rethink his finances and where it came from. When he did again impose a tax in 1512 he restricted it to clergy only. By that time he was much better placed financially and was receiving funds from other sources. In 1497 the Archbishop of St Andrews, William Scheve, died and James replaced him with his brother James, Duke of Ross, who would have been about 20 at the time.

For the king this brought many benefits. The canonical age of consecration was at that time 27, so for the next seven years archiepiscopal revenues would pass instead to the king. It also meant that, with the king having this control over his younger brother, there was less chance of Ross being used by rebels wanting to place him on the throne instead of his brother. This was a move which was well thought out.

James's finances improved further the following year when he reached the age of 25. This was the age when he was legally allowed to revoke all grants made during his minority. But while this would have boosted his income considerably, it was also likely to anger too many people so instead he focused on receiving extra income from people to receive royal confirmation of their holdings.

When his brother the Duke of Ross died suddenly in January 1504, still unconsecrated, the king passed the title to his 11-year-old son, Alexander Stewart. Again, revenues passed directly to the king until the boy reached the age of 27.

James was a king who travelled his country more than most kings before or after him and he was known for visiting villages and towns throughout the land, often sleeping in simple dwelling places as opposed to large castles. But for most of the year he could be found either in Edinburgh, Stirling or Linlithgow. In the early years of his reign he spent Christmas at Linlithgow, after that he preferred Edinburgh.

Before his marriage he tended to spend Lent in Stirling, at the convent of the Observantine Friars, where he would dress in the brown robes of the Order. Many of the theological and philosophical books he bought were for the friary.

James loved horses and dogs, shooting with the crossbow or longbow and playing tennis. He was a very accomplished horseman and it was said that he could ride from Stirling to Aberdeen and then on to Elgin in one day.

He also loved hawks and once paid £180 for a single hawk. Every year he spent a large amount of money buying hawks or rewarding those who brought hawks to him as gifts, or on the expenses of falconers sent out to capture hawks. It was normal for his falconers to accompany him on his journeys, even when he went on pilgrimages to St Ninians or St Duthac.

In the evenings when he was staying at one of his castles the king would have supper, eating with his hands as cutlery was still to come to Scotland, before playing cards or backgammon. He had his own musicians he could call on – trumpeters, drummers and fiddlers, as well as four Italian minstrels.

The evening might also include dancers and acrobats, a storyteller or a play. If he was travelling and staying at the house of a wealthy landowner, he would welcome an unknown entertainer and would reward him appropriately.

We are lucky in that de Ayala observed and noted much of what he saw at the Scottish court and he has left us with a pretty full picture of what James was like. He builds a picture of a devout man and tells us that the king did not eat meat on Wednesdays or Fridays, he wouldn't ride a horse on Sundays, even to go to Mass, and that before conducting any serious business he heard two masses.

At least once a year he made pilgrimages to St Ninians in Galloway and St Duthac at Tain. During Holy Week he could be found at the Observantine Friary in Stirling, sharing the fasts and vigils of the friars.

He was keen to invest in the country, to improve the castles and palaces and make them something to be proud of. At the start of his reign Falkland was a mere hunting lodge, set in the centre of a game reserve. It provided food for the royal table at Holyrood House. James began the erection of the new palace, which his son James V continued.

Between 1501 and 1505 he built a new Gothic palace at Holyrood, and it was here he married Margaret Tudor in 1503. Today only the tower remains. While his son, James V, added to the palace, it was burnt down in 1544 during the war of the Rough

Wooing and again in 1559. Cromwell's soldiers burnt the rest down in 1650.

Linlithgow Palace was a stopping off place between Stirling and Edinburgh and during his reign James IV significantly added to it. James gave the palace to Margaret as a wedding present and it was here she waited in vain for his return in 1513. Today the palace still stands but is roofless, a fire in 1746 having destroyed much of the building.

Stirling Castle is the royal residence most associated with James IV. He was responsible for the King's Old Building, completed around 1497 as a new residence for the king. Next, he built the Great Hall, described as the 'grandest secular building erected in Scotland in the late Middle Ages'. It was the first Renaissance-influenced royal architecture in Scotland and James employed English craftsmen to work on it and to incorporate English ideas. Finally, in 1501 he had the collegiate chapel built, and it was here in 1543 that his granddaughter Mary, Queen of Scots was crowned.

Far from faultless, James emerged from his minority as someone we could describe as an intriguing character. His motives, both in harbouring Perkin Warbeck and in attacking England, were questionable. But he was a strong leader, who sought to make peace within Scotland and who took steps to bring Scotland up to speed with the rest of Europe.

Chapter 5

Women In His Life

An important aspect of the life of any Scottish king, and of most kings in fact, was their mistresses. They may not have played a part in public life, at least not formally, but they could have an effect on who gained power and influence with the king, and often the family of the king's mistress would see their fortunes rise as he ensured that the family of his present loved one were looked after. It was for this reason that ruthless families were often very keen to put forward a young girl from their family, in the hope of making her the king's mistress. A perfect example of this was Henry VIII, where on several occasions the king's mistress, and at times his wife, were central to a family's manipulative plan to gain power and favour.

The fate of the woman after the romance had ended was in many ways decided by the king. Often, she would be married off to a Scottish nobleman, who would accept any of the king's children, not as his own, but as part of his wife's family. This is in contrast to other unmarried mothers who would have found it hard to find someone to take them and their children on. The king's children tended to be well looked after, both as children and in adulthood. Their needs would be met financially, and the king would see to it that a suitable career or marriage was arranged.

James was no exception. He was known to have four mistresses, before and after his marriage to Margaret Tudor, and fathered at least seven illegitimate children. Most likely there were other dalliances along the way, but it is the story of the other Margaret in his life which has fascinated people for centuries.

The other Margaret was Margaret Drummond, and the story is one of a possible secret marriage, accusations of poisoning and of a king heartbroken at the loss of his one true love.

Margaret Drummond was the daughter of John Drummond, first Lord Drummond, and Lady Elizabeth Lindsay, and was the great-great-great-great-niece of David II's second wife Margaret Drummond. Born near Crieff, it is not known when exactly her romance with the king began, but there is a record of her living in Stirling Castle in June 1496, and in spring 1497 she was residing at Linlithgow Palace. Certainly, James had visited her family home of Drummond Castle on 25 April 1496, but the affair may have started as early as 1495, as her father was at this time made justiciar, which suggests that by this point they were involved enough that she could either influence the king's decisions enough to raise her father to this position or new love had made him want to reward her family in some way. Possibly it was a bit of both.

The poem Tayis Bank is often accredited to James, reputedly a love poem written for Margaret. While a king would often have one main mistress while still visiting other women, with Margaret this was not the case and it is believed that he stayed true to her, for the time he was with her at least. They were said to be very much in love and had wed in secret, waiting for dispensation from the pope in order to make the marriage public.

But then in 1501 Margaret and two of her sisters, Euphemia and Sybilla, died suddenly at their parents' home. It was said that they had been poisoned, having all eaten the same food in the morning.

If one takes into account the poor standards of hygiene in the day fatal food poisoning is entirely feasible and was not uncommon at the time. James paid for masses to be said for her soul for several years afterwards and continued to support their daughter Margaret financially, moving her from Drummond Castle to Stirling Castle.

That is one version of what happened. Another, a more sinister version, has Margaret and her sisters dying, not from accidental food poisoning but from being murdered by English agents, keen to get her out of the way so that the king would marry Margaret

Tudor. If the king had in fact married Margaret Drummond, then he would need to be freed from her to allow him to marry again.

Margaret's uncle was Walter Drummond, Dean of Dunblane, and it was at the cathedral in Dunblane that the Drummond sisters were buried. You can visit the cathedral today and see the plaque commemorating them, which reads:

In memory of Margaret, eldest daughter of John, 1st Lord Drummond, by tradition privately married to King James IV and poisoned at Drummond Castle with her sisters Euphemia and Sybilla by some of the nobles who desired the king's marriage with Princess Margaret of England. The three sisters were buried beneath these slabs in the choir of the cathedral of which their uncle Walter was dean. AD1501.

A quick look on the official website of the British Monarchy confirms this story.

So, we have two supposedly reliable sources stating that the Drummond sisters were poisoned, in order to allow the king to marry the English Margaret Tudor, with one source saying that Margaret Drummond and King James were actually more than lovers and were in fact married. Was this the case? Did the king marry a woman who would have been considered a commoner, preferring to do this than to make an international alliance with King Henry VII of England? Did he love Margaret Drummond enough that he was prepared to bear the results of Henry's rage at his daughter being rejected for a common Scots woman?

Most historians agree that the answer to these questions is no. James was far too wise a man to let love stand in the way of making a marriage which would benefit him politically in Europe. He had already agreed to the marriage and there is no evidence that he attempted to get out of it. Scotland was a much smaller and less important country than England and if anyone was likely to have wanted to get out of the marriage it would have been the English.

The suggestion that Margaret Drummond and James were already married but were awaiting dispensation from the pope in order to make the marriage public also has no bearings on reality. The pair were indeed related, but not closely enough that they would require permission from the pope in order to marry.

It is highly unlikely that agents, whether they were English or not, would feel the need to kill Margaret and her sisters. And there is no evidence that the king knew of these rumours and considered it worth having them investigated.

In fact, the rumour appears to have started as late as the seventeenth century with Viscount Strathallen (William Drummond) writing a eulogistic history of his family. And it has continued ever since as it is a sad but romantic story – of a king and his one true love; who was prepared to go against what his country would have expected of him and insult the great Henry Tudor; of a young girl and her sisters who died so that they would not get in the way. And of a heartbroken king who never forgot her. It's a good story and one for Hollywood perhaps, but is unlikely to have any truth in it.

Another story has it that Janet Kennedy, James's next mistress, was involved in her death. This story, which has been put around over the centuries, by supporters of the Drummonds, and by those who like a good murder mystery, has it that the king had now fallen for Janet Kennedy, and, in order to get rid of her rival, Janet was the instigator in having Margaret Drummond murdered.

This is also unlikely. There is certainly no evidence to support this theory, and it is likely that it was simply gossip, which people chose to repeat over the years. It makes a good story and that is all it likely is – a made-up story. But Margaret Drummond was certainly not the king's first mistress. Marion Boyd, daughter of Archibald Boyd and Christine Mure, was the king's first known mistress, the relationship lasting from 1492 to 1495 and, like Margaret Drummond her family, benefited from the liaison, with her uncle the Earl of Angus being chancellor from 1493 to 1498. James fathered three children with her, two of whom, Alexander and Catherine, lived to adulthood.

Alexander would later become Archbishop of St Andrews, and James was known to be extremely proud of his eldest son. He was educated in France, Italy and the Low Countries, before going to Padua to be educated by Erasmus. He returned to Scotland in 1510 and became Lord Chancellor of Scotland at the age of 17. The following year he co-founded St Leonard's College in St Andrews. He died fighting for his father at Flodden, and his old tutor Erasmus wrote a moving obituary of him.

Once the relationship with Marion had run its course, the king arranged for her to marry John Muire of Rowallan, and provided her with a generous annuity, as well as giving her some land in Ayrshire. James would always acknowledge and look after his illegitimate children and likewise he ensured that his mistresses were looked after too.

The Tudor Stewart marriage in 1503 did nothing to stop the king's roving eye, neither would it have been expected to. Kings were expected to have mistresses throughout their marriage, and nobody would have thought anything of it. Mistresses saw to the king's sexual desires when the queen was pregnant, but in an era where royalty married for influence and power and not love, having a mistress was viewed more as a social pastime, something kings and princes did for relaxation, as opposed to adultery. Most queens accepted it without a fight, and most decent kings did not flaunt their mistresses or illegitimate children in front of them.

Janet Kennedy was born some time before 1483 so was a few years younger than the king. Through her father she was the great-great-granddaughter of Robert III. The affair began in 1499 and continued after his marriage. Janet had previously been the Earl of Angus's mistress, an enemy of the king's at this time, but this did not seem to bother anyone when she moved from Angus to the king. She was the mistress of four men in total, at least two of whom died with the king at Flodden.

Records tell us that the king would usually combine his pilgrimages to Tain with visits to Janet at Darnaway, and he did this the autumn after his wedding. In April 1503 she was at Bothwell and James visited her there on his way to Whithorn.

Margaret Drummond may have been the most famous of James's mistresses, but Janet Kennedy was the longest lasting. The king gave her Darnaway Castle on condition that she remained unmarried. She bore him three children – Jane, Margaret and James

Stewart, first Earl of Moray.

Later came Lady Agnes Stewart, or Isabella as she was sometimes known. The daughter of James Stewart, first Earl of Buchan and his wife Margaret, Agnes Stewart was married four times in total. Little is known of her relationship with James, but we know it began some time before 1511 and that they had a daughter together, Janet. She became known as 'La Belle Ecossaise', was Mary Queen of Scots' governess, and her daughter Mary was one of the 'four Marys' whom the queen played with.

James spent time with these women. He may have been in love with some of them and he certainly fathered children with them, but in reality marriage to one of them was never a realistic prospect. It is unlikely that any of his mistresses even considered this. They would have known the rules of society and knew that the country would not accept a commoner as queen.

In any case marriage negotiations had been on the cards for James for the majority of his life. As a baby he had been promised to Lady Cecilia, youngest daughter of Edward IV, and in October 1474 ambassadors from England had arrived in Scotland with the Earl of Crawford taking the marriage vows on behalf of the one-year-old prince and clasping the hands of Lord Scope who replied on behalf of the three-year-old princess.

The treaty of marriage was signed on 26 October and was ratified by the Scottish king on 3 November. James, then Duke of Rothesay, was to marry the Lady Cecilia within six months of his coming of proper age, and a dowry of 20,000 marks was to be paid over a period of 17 years.

But as anyone with a good knowledge of English history will know, this was a period of much upheaval in England. Edward IV died in 1483 and Richard III soon seized the throne from his nephew Edward V.

In September 1484 a contract was signed, preparing for the marriage of James to Anne de la Pole, niece of Richard III. Commissioners were sent south to meet Richard's representatives in York and to complete the arrangements. But Richard's death at the Battle of Bosworth in 1485 put an end to these plans.

Shortly after the death of his mother, James was again involved in another marriage negotiation with England which involved his brother marrying and his father remarrying. Interestingly James, although the heir to the throne and the eldest son, was to marry an unnamed daughter of the late King Edward, while his brother, his father's favourite son, was to marry Edward IV's daughter the Lady Katharine. James III was to marry Queen Elizabeth, Edward IV's widow.

Again, the death of a king ended these negotiations. This time it was the death of King James III in 1488 which totally changed things. With his new position as king, as opposed to heir apparent, he was in a better place to negotiate a marriage treaty.

Later, during the time of Perkin Warbeck, and as part of peace negotiations, Henry offered his distant kinswoman the Lady Katherine, Countess of Wiltshire, to the Scottish king, but James would only marry a real princess. One wonders whether Henry was trying to antagonise his neighbour.

Again, as part of peace negotiations in 1496 Henry Tudor offered his daughter Margaret as wife to the Scottish king. Margaret was only six years old at the time and far too young to marry. It was likely that this was just a ploy by Henry VII and at the time he did not consider the agreement binding. There were, after all, more marriageable men about. But after all the failed marriage negotiations over the years this one did take place and, while the mistresses came and went, Margaret Tudor, as queen of Scotland, stayed and outlived the king.

Chapter 6

Building Up The Navy

Many an older Glaswegian will speak woefully of the 'good old days' when Glasgow was king of the shipbuilding industry, lamenting the time when the city's shipyards supplied ships to countries across the globe.

This may have been the golden era of the shipbuilding world in the twentieth century, but for the Scottish navy the reign of James IV was the time when life had never been so good. This was the heyday of the Scots royal navy. Long before Britannia ruled the waves, Scottish ships were impressing Europe. Towards the end of his reign James's greatest expenditure was on ships and their maintenance, and his naval programme was very impressive, particularly when you consider the small size of the country.

When in August 1506 James wrote to Louis XII of France that the building of a fleet to defend Scotland was a project he meant to see through he certainly meant it. During the 25 years he was king he built, bought, hired, was given and seized 38 ships, a complete change from the situation of the fifteenth century when the Scottish navy was practically non-existent.

The situation in England had not been much better. Henry Tudor had seven ships at the start of his reign. This had been reduced to five by 1488 and had only increased to seven again by the time of Henry VIII's accession in 1509. This from a country which was bigger in size and population than Scotland, and which importantly was an island country.

The reason for Scotland failing to have a navy of any size was partly down to insufficient funds, and partly due to a lack of need for much of the past hundred years. Scotland's main enemy, England, was at peace with Scotland for most of the time, with no major invasions at all until the 1480s. That is not to say that all was peaceful. In the 1470s there were a couple of incidents. One of Sir John Colquhoun of Luss's ships was captured by a ship belonging to Lord Grey. And Sir Andrew Wood's ship the *Yellow Carvel*, which historians believe was part-owned by the king, was seized by seamen working for the Duke of Gloucester.

The problem did become less immediate when Edward IV died in 1483. The next couple of years were marked by internal politics in England – the non-existent reign and then disappearance of the young Edward V, and the belligerent two years of Richard III's reign which ended with his death at the Battle of Bosworth. Even Henry Tudor, when he came to power, did not make the navy a priority.

But when attacks did eventually come it highlighted how bad the Scottish navy actually was. In 1481 when England's Lord Howard raided the coast of the Firth of Forth, he burnt the town of Blackness and seized eight small ships and one large ship from various locations along the coastline. Sir Andrew Wood tried to retaliate, and did inflict some damage, but his own ship also suffered damage.

Then during the Albany rebellion of 1482, when Gloucester and Albany attacked Scotland with their army, they were backed up by Sir Robert Radcliff, who, with a large fleet of ships, sailed as far in as Leith. This resulted in them losing Berwick to the English for the last time, and losing Dunbar, which was not recovered for another four years. It was starting to become obvious that Scotland was in no place to defend its seas and should war with England break out again Scotland would be in no state to retaliate at sea.

When James first came to power this would all have been recent history. But he was also aware that Scottish merchants needed to be protected at sea. Scotland had been leaving itself open to attack on the seas for too long. The Firth of Forth had long been susceptible to attack at the hands of the English and other pirates, and so in

1491 parliament granted to John Dundas and his heirs the island and rock of Inchgarvie near Queensferry, with the powers to erect a castle or fortalice to defend the firth.

James set out to build a navy that would impress. In July 1504 a Breton merchant was paid £100 for a ship. He also commissioned the French shipwright Martin Le Nault to build a larger ship, costing £1,085 and named the *Treasurer*. He had able captains, including John Barton and his three sons Robert, John and Andrew, but was short of shipbuilders so John Lorans and Jennen Diew were brought over from France to work on building the *Margaret*. James also looked to France for wood and before his arrival in Scotland Diew had been employed by James to choose French wood to take to Scotland. There had been a shortage of hard wood in Scotland and by 1503 often it had to be imported.

One name that comes up time and time again in the latter part of the fifteenth century is that of Sir Andrew Wood, sometimes called the Scottish Nelson. He may have helped James III try to escape the rebels in 1488 but it was under the reign of James IV that he really made his name. During the period of 1489–90 he was involved in at least one sea fight with the English, which he won. The king responded by knighting him, while Henry VII, on the other hand, offered £1,000 a year for any English captain who captured Wood.

At the May 1491 parliament Wood's feu-charter of Largo was confirmed, and he was told that it would not be affected by any future royal revocation. They also gave him a licence for the work he had already done there, building houses as well as a fortalice to defend Largo from attack from pirates and other invaders. Wood was the kind of man the Scottish Parliament needed and wanted to keep.

In August 1506 James promised King Louis that the Scottish fleet would be there to help France whenever she needed it. The 1502 Treaty of Perpetual Peace with England was still relatively new, and rather than directly attack England, the alliance with France could provide James with the opportunity to annoy Henry Tudor, without directly going to war. Certainly, France provided much of the timber for James's ships; they were largely built by

Scottish shipwrights, and France also provided much of the finance. It is quite conceivable that Louis of France had an alternative reason for being so helpful.

At the start of James's reign, the west coast, specifically Dumbarton, was where ships were built but after a few years this had moved to the east coast. The *Margaret* was built in Leith, completed two years after the king's marriage to Margaret Tudor, with the ship named after her.

Her size meant that a special dock had to be built at Leith before construction could begin, adding to the cost, which eventually came to £8,000, a large chunk of the king's income. The ship had four masts, was 600 to 700 tonnes, similar in size to the English *Mary Rose*, and was at this time the largest ship in the Scottish navy. Wood had been used from Kincardine, Alloa and Strathearn, as well as from France and Norway. At the end of every stage of her construction there was celebrations with minstrels and trumpeters – when she was taken off the stocks in dry docks, when the mainmast was raised, and of course on the floating of the ship. Even before she had been floated, the king would go down to Leith to dine on board, with the place decorated for the occasion, with tapestries and silver plates brought from Edinburgh. On her maiden voyage in the summer of June 1506 James sailed out to the Isle of May.

When his uncle, King John of Denmark, requested help in 1505, James made excuses, saying that he couldn't give him the two ships he asked for as the larger ships he had were still in the builders' yard, while others were being repaired. Others had been detained in Brittany. It is no surprise that James was a bit reticent. His previous efforts to help his uncle in 1502 had been a disaster. King John of Denmark had called on his nephew to help him when the Swedes and some of the Norwegian aristocracy had risen up against him, and some important castles had been captured. The Scottish fleet was too small, and they were far too ill prepared. Many Scots were killed in Denmark, and back home people were very reluctant to pay the Danish tax. James did not make the same mistake twice.

Meanwhile James was becoming dissatisfied with Leith as a shipbuilding port. It has been suggested that this was because of the sandbanks at the mouth of the water, which had caused problems when sailing the *Margaret* out to sea.

James had recently visited New Haven and decided that it was suitable for a new dockyard. Craftsmen from France, Spain, Flanders and Denmark were shipped in, with local artificers and labourers brought in to help.

However, this still didn't solve the problem of the ships being built in places where they were exposed to attack, so next James ordered the construction of another dockyard at Pool of Airth, near Stirling. The waters here were large and the *Margaret* stayed there for the winter of 1507–8.

Another ship, the self-titled *James*, cost the king £65. It wasn't a large ship, and it is thought that when it was bought it needed refitting, hence why James bought it at a reduced price.

But it was the ship the *Great Michael* which was the proudest naval achievement of his reign. It is often said that the building of the *Great Michael* used all the wood in Fife, apart from Falkland. In fact, timber from Norway was also used. It would have needed a lot of wood for it was a very big ship. Measuring 120 feet by 36 feet (Pitscottie gives longer measurements which are not credible), it was the largest warship in Europe at the time, twice the original displacement of the English ship the *Mary Rose*, and big enough that the whole of Christopher Columbus's fleet that sailed to the New World could have fitted into the hull.

Its walls were said to be ten feet thick, so strong it was said that no cannon could get through it and there were six cannons on each side. There have been various accounts giving details of the ship, but they tend to be unreliable sources who are suspected of exaggerating, making it hard to know exactly what the ship looked like.

James was keen to see how the work was going and spent much time at Leith overseeing the project. Official records tell us that Margaret paid him a surprise visit in October 1511. They ate a meal together and spent the night there.

James was very proud of the *Great Michael* and it went a good way towards increasing his standing in Europe. Another reason he wanted to build up a navy was because he needed ships for the Crusades. A devout Christian in many ways, James was keen to take part in the Crusades, although his early death meant that he never got the chance, and he had men in nearly every country in Western Europe buying timber for production of the Scottish navy.

Through necessity James had to rely on part ownership or hiring of merchants' ships, particularly in the early years of his reign. One of the three Barton brothers – Robert Barton – was paid £150 for half of one of his ships.

On 12 October 1511 the *Great Michael* was launched at Newhaven, with as much fanfare and celebrations as the *Margaret*. The next four months were spent fitting the boat out, and she wasn't towed out into the Forth until February 1512. That month the king dined on her and the following month he sailed to Queensferry on the *Great Michael*. From there she was towed to Pool of Airth for further outfitting.

Certainly by 1513 his plans were starting to come together. He now had four large ships – the *Margaret*, the *Great Michael*, the *James* and the *Treasurer*. On 20 March he bought *The Barque of Abberville* from France for £300. This he added to his rather small-scale fleet of smaller ships. Additionally, he had some ships for special tasks and some raw barges. The king enjoyed dining on his large ships and was proud to have them to show off.

The Bartons, Wood, Brownhill, Chalmers and Falconer all privately owned ships which the king hired when required. It was a bit of a makeshift army, but it was sufficient enough for his needs and certainly helped improve his standing internationally, as well as helping protect Scottish seamen.

The Bartons had always served the king well. Robert Barton was employed by James to bring timber and skilled craftsmen to Leith, Newhaven and Pool of Airth. John, his brother, was given the job of taking James's eldest son Alexander Stewart, Archbishop of St Andrews, to France in September 1507 on board the *Treasurer*, and by 1512 he was in command of the *Margaret*.

The third brother, Andrew, was given lands in Fife by James, worth a considerable amount in annual income. And it was Andrew, in particular, who developed a reputation in England and Portugal as a pirate.

In July 1507 as a thank you for his services James renewed letters of marque against the Portuguese which James III had previously granted to Andrew's father but which had since been suspended. The letters authorised Barton to attack any Portuguese vessel he met and allowed him to take the ship and cargo as payback for a crime committed by the Portuguese in the 1470s when, while trading in Flanders, John Barton's ships had been attacked by Portuguese vessels.

This was worth a considerable amount for Andrew Barton but was also highly dangerous and the following year Barton was arrested by the Dutch authorities at Veere, having tried to capture a Dutch ship. King James had to intervene and speak to Maximilian, the Holy Roman Emperor, and others on his behalf.

The following year Barton was in trouble again when he tried the same thing again, this time with a Portuguese ship carrying English cargo. In December 1509 Barton appeared before the Lord of Council having been sued by the merchants whose goods he had stolen. In the summer of 1510 James, having received complaints from the Portuguese king, felt that he had to take action, and suspended the letters of marque for a year.

Barton's reputation certainly went before him. King John of Denmark, still trying to persuade James to send help for his fight against the Swedes and Lubeckers, started to ask specifically for Andrew and Robert Barton. Robert Barton did sail to Denmark, with his brother Andrew following a year or two later, probably to avoid trouble. In March he had been summoned to answer charges that he had seized a Breton ship and had stolen goods from some Antwerp merchants. His piracy activities had reached new heights, and even King James was getting fed up with him. In July 1511 the king refused to renew the letters of marque.

In late summer 1511 Sir Edward Howard, while being paid by King Henry to protect the English seas, came upon Barton and his two ships, the *Lion* and the *Jennet of Purwyn*, and a battle ensued.

Barton was killed, his ships were taken and his men were taken prisoner.

James complained to his brother-in-law and demanded that the crews be released. Andrew Barton may have been a bit of a wild cat in latter years, but he was a friend of the king's and they would sometimes play cards together. But the king was also realistic about the situation and he appears to have moved on and accepted the reality pretty quickly.

Why was James so determined to pursue a large Scottish navy? If one looks at various aspects of his reign and policy during that time he was certainly determined to leave Scotland in a better position than it was when he came to power. It would not be too unreasonable that a king, who was determined to improve the education of his people, who made a good choice of bride, and who united a divided nation, should also make such efforts on the international front.

But some historians have been sceptical of his motives, and the percentage of his income which he spent on the navy was on the high side, suggesting that this was a priority for him. One theory put forward is that, as the navy was largely built with French wood, by French workmen, and financed by France, he was doing it, in part for France's benefit should it need the ships, but also as a way of attacking England without breaking the Treaty of Perpetual Peace.

The *Great Michael*, for its part, was sold to King Louis XII of France in April 1514 for a mere 40,000 livres, just a few months after King James died at Flodden. In France she was renamed *La Grande Nef d'Ecosse* (The Big Nave of Scotland), and as in Scotland where her size caused some problems, she had to rest in Honfleur because she was too big for the harbour at Dieppe.

What happened to her next is now under dispute. It has long been believed that, as reported by the Scottish historian George Buchanan, she was left to rot at Brest. However, a more recent theory is that *La Grande Nef d'Ecosse* took part in the French attack on England in 1545, the attack which led to the sinking of Henry VIII's ship the *Mary Rose*.

Whatever his motives for spending so much on the navy were, it was on land rather than at sea where the action was in 1513, when events finally came to a head. France did indeed have a part to play in the events of the following year, but it was Scotland that suffered.

Chapter 7

The Man Behind The Monarch

The Renaissance King is a title often given to James IV and not just because of the era in which he lived. During his reign Scotland got caught up in the changes sweeping Europe and in many ways it marched on, rather than simply being influenced by changes elsewhere. Some of these changes happened naturally and can't be accredited to anything James did or anything he sanctioned, but the majority were as a result of James initiating change and he was certainly at the helm of many of the developments going on.

His support of both the arts and science in his own country reaffirms the assertion that he was well deserved of the title, and he is often credited with taking Scotland out of the Middle Ages, bringing it up in line with England and the rest of Europe, and in some respects overtaking these countries. He was a king who not only ruled but who energised the country.

Let's go back to the beginning of James's reign. In 1488 he was still just a boy of 15. While this can't fairly be compared with a fifteen-year-old in today's society, then 15-year-olds could marry, and in effect could rule unaided should they insist, in many ways he was still a boy and it was to be some time before he ruled on his own.

Like many 15-year-olds he wanted to have fun and enjoy himself and as we saw earlier it was this love of fun and of having a good time that worried his lords. While the lords' worries were unfounded, and he did soon settle down to business, he continued to enjoy himself long after he had left boyhood. Crowds of people, including knights from foreign countries, would flock to Edinburgh for the tournaments, jousting and trials of strength which would often take place.

The treasurer's accounts provide plenty of examples of money given to the Moors for various reasons. The Moors were indigenous black Europeans who for many years had been high-ranking people present in the royal courts of Europe. Many were artists and singers, others were scholars, alchemists and astrologers.

One was a drummer who accompanied James on his tours of the Highlands. The records show that the king bought a horse for him and paid for his drum to be painted.

Moorish women were also part of court life and were treated well. The accounts give examples of money given to them for new gowns and for material for dresses. Other entries simply state the amount given and who the money was for.

James appears to have been very accepting of these foreigners. The Moorish people continued to play a part in court life but after his death in 1513 they start to appear less in the accounts.

Perhaps because he was fully aware of how unstable a throne could be, he was keen to be well liked by the people, rich and poor. He regularly consulted with his lords and took their advice, but he was also keen to be liked by the common people.

Often he would ride alone around the country. In disguise and without letting on who he was he would ask the country folk what the king was like, what kind of man he was and what was said of him, hence gleaning the most honest of reports.

At this time in Scotland there were only inns in the large towns, but James was happy enough to stay in an alehouse or in one of his subjects' houses, where he would give the family a small fee for their services.

Contemporary reports of him were very positive. Erasmus, the tutor of James's eldest illegitimate son, describes the king as having a 'wonderful force of intellect, and an incredible knowledge of all things'.

According to the Spanish ambassador Pedro de Ayala, who admittedly may have exaggerated a bit, James could speak very good Latin, as well as having good French, German, Flemish,

Italian and Spanish. He was very complimentary about the king, describing him as a man who feared God and observed all the rituals of the Church and gave alms to the poor.

However, he also described him as a vain man, who acted like he was king of the world and not just of Scotland.

James was also said to be able to speak some Gaelic, the language of the people in the Highlands and Islands. This may have helped keep the islanders in line. De Ayala described them as warlike and agile but said that under James IV's reign they were now kept in line in a way that previous kings could not do.

As well as describing King James, Ayala described the people. The Scots, he described as loving war, saying that if there was no war, they simply fought with each other. But he noted that they had learned that James IV wasn't afraid to execute the law, saying that Scotland had improved so much under his rule that it was now worth three times more than before. Certainly, Spaniards living in Flanders reported increased trade with Scotland.

Keen to put his father's death in the past, and the troubles which caused it, James wanted a peaceful country and he was keen to bring law and order to his kingdom. In 1493, five years into his reign and with no sign of any more rebellions, he restored the 'justice ayre' which had fallen away during the reign of his grandfather James II. These were regional courts which were held twice a year in all the major towns and James personally presided over each of them.

According to the historian, Robert Lindsay of Pitscottie, the king was so skilled in surgery that other surgeons looked to him for advice. While this may appear a pretty strong claim, there is plenty of evidence that he certainly was experienced in performing surgery. In the treasurer's accounts for that period, there are many entries detailing monies paid to people in order for the king to perform simple operations such as bloodletting or teeth extraction, with dentistry being a particular favourite. For example, in 1491 he paid a man 28 shillings for letting him take blood. In 1503 he bought 'one turcas to tak out teith'. A turcas was an instrument of torture.

In April 1501 the treasurer's accounts show that 14 shillings was given to a woman who had been blinded, probably from James trying to cure a cataract unsuccessfully.

James had a very inquisitive mind and his position allowed him to take advantage of the opportunities the common man wouldn't have had. He was particularly interested in medical matters, and as well as doing a bit of experimenting himself, he showed his support to those in the profession.

While this could be viewed as a sign that had he not been king or had he been born a few hundred years later he could perhaps have entered the medical profession, in reality it was probably more related to his love of tournaments. He would often join in tournaments incognito, on foot and on horseback. The treasurer's accounts tell us he was wounded in at least one tournament. There is mention of 'half an elne of kersay' to support the king's hand, 'an elne of silk for a bandage' and 'five quarters of taffeta' to support his hand.

In the Middle Ages it was common for knights to pick up a bit of surgical knowledge in preparation for when they would need it.

Pitscottie also reports of some unusual social experiments. He tells the tale of two brothers born in Glasgow about 1490 with two bodies separated only from the waist up. They could walk and had their own personalities, indeed often arguing amongst themselves. When he found out about them James was fascinated and he brought the children to court in order to be able to educate them and to study them more.

Educated in English, Irish, French, Italian, Spanish, Danish, and Dutch, the boys became accomplished musicians, as well as singing duets. Both boys lived to the age of 28, when they died within days of each other.

The human mind, as well as the human body, obviously fascinated him. Another of his experiments involved sending a dumb woman to the island of Inchkeith with two very young children, to see what language they would speak when they grew up. He wanted to find out what the original language was. Pitscottie says, 'Some say they spak guid Hebrew. But as to myself I knew not.' Other sources, including Sir Walter Scott, agree that it was highly unlikely they would have been able to speak any proper language.

James encouraged the study of alchemy during his reign, but it is thought that this interest was financially motivated, rather than scientifically. As a king who liked to both play and work hard, there were costs to be met.

In the treasurer's accounts there are also several examples of payments made to alchemists, and of purchases made of tools. He established laboratories and furnaces at Stirling and Linlithgow, but there is no evidence of any production.

In a letter to the king of Denmark James speaks of a John Haboch, a goldwasher who had been in Scotland and who would 'give him an account of minerals of Scotland, particularly gold'.

It was his court alchemist and physician, the Italian John Damian, who was involved in another of James's experiments, perhaps to gain favour after his repeated attempts to make gold. In what certainly must have been one of the earliest recorded attempts at flying, Damian made a pair of wings and attempted to fly from the walls of Stirling Castle to France. He landed at the foot of the rock and ended up with a broken thigh. It was reported that the king ran down afterwards, a fair distance, and was met with Damian's excuse that he had used the wrong type of feathers.

But the legendary 'Birdman of Stirling' stayed in the king's favour, despite the experiment failing. In 1504 James made him Abbot of Tungland in Galloway, and although he went to study abroad for five years, he returned to the king in Scotland and continued working at the court until the king died in 1513.

For his time the king was also advanced in his thoughts and beliefs on personal hygiene. On 22 September 1497 he issued through the Privy Council an Act stating that all those suffering from grandgore (the Scottish name for syphilis) should assemble at Leith, where boats would take them to Inchkeith and other islands in the firth until they were better.

He was a man ahead of his time, in an age where it was still common for people to only have a bath once or twice a year, and where medics advised people that it was dangerous to wash the face as it could cause catarrh or weaken the eyesight.

He considered isolation important. Plague stricken people were to be housebound with no contact with the healthy unless carrying a white stick or wearing a piece of white cloth on their clothes. Infected houses were to be marked with cloth draped across the entrance or stairway. Dogs, cats and pigs found wandering the streets were to be destroyed.

In 1498 legislation was brought in to say that nobody was to harbour strangers or to import goods from suspected or infected areas. More than 150 years later, during the Great Plague of London, it was the importing of a bundle of cloth which was to bring the disease to the town of Eyam in Derbyshire.

A 10pm curfew was introduced except for lawful errands and no child under the age of 13 was to be allowed to roam the streets alone at night.

But James also made changes to the judicial system in Scotland, realising that there was a need for a full judicial review.

On 13 June 1496, eight years into his reign, he sought to tackle the issue of there being a lack of well-trained judges. In this year legislation was passed in what could be described as the first Scottish education Act. Under this Act, all landowners were legally obliged to send their eldest son to grammar school when they were eight or nine years old and to keep them there until they were 'competentlie foundit and have perfect latyn and theraftir to remain three years at the sculis of art and jure, sua that thai may have knowledge and understanding of the lawis. Throw the quikris justice may reign universalie throw all the realme'.

Anyone who failed to do this without a lawful excuse was liable to pay the court £20 Scots.

The aim of the Act was to ensure that sheriffs and all those involved in enforcing and upholding the law would have the knowledge and understanding needed to do their jobs. Considering that it would be another four hundred years before England introduced its first education Act, in many ways James was ahead of his time.

In July 1505 he granted the Seal of Cause to the Barber-Surgeons of Edinburgh, the predecessor of the Royal College of Surgeons of Edinburgh. In those days being a barber was a slightly different job to what it is today, and they dabbled in medical matters. This Seal of Cause allowed them to perform dissections and formalised their role as a Craft Guild of the City. It set appropriate examination standards for all prospective candidates and included a request to be given the dead body of a criminal once a year in order to practise. It was a kind of seal of approval from the king but also an opportunity to take things a step further. For his time this was very forward thinking. Although dissections were carried out in some European cities, Edinburgh was the first city in Britain to allow them. It was another 35 years before such a step was taken in London.

In September of this year, King's College, Aberdeen, obtained its charter and offered medicine as a subject of study. Aberdeen became the first university in Scotland to have a separate medical facility and to admit members of the laity, while also becoming the first medical school in Britain.

The birth of Aberdeen University had begun more than ten years prior to this when William Elphinstone, Bishop of Aberdeen, became appalled at the people of Aberdeen and their lack of education, describing them as barbarous.

Elphinstone had been born and educated in Glasgow and had studied for a time in Paris. He became aware that neither of the Scottish universities, Glasgow or St Andrews, had a school of civil law, so ambitious theologians had to travel to Paris or Orleans to further their studies.

In 1495, with the king's approval, he obtained a papal bull from Pope Alexander VI allowing him to provide a *studium generale* (the old name for a medieval university where international students, as opposed to just local students, were welcome to study). The new university was to provide undergraduate courses in theology, medicine, and canon and civil law, and would be open to all, not just the clergy.

The king donated some money and in 1498 a royal charter made

Aberdeen the seat of a university. Two years later building began, although teaching had been going on for some time. By 1506 the work was complete and what was to become known as King's College, in recognition of the part King James played, was opened.

So, while in Edinburgh the foundations had been put in place for more formalised medical dissections, in Aberdeen the establishment of a new university was to ensure that, rather than being left behind with regards to education, Scotland was going to show Europe that it was a country worth watching.

But despite it now having three universities, and an increasing need for books following the education Act, progress was being held back due to one omission – the printing press. All books had to either be handwritten or imported from England or Europe, where printing had already been established.

So, in September 1507 James issued a warrant to allow textile merchant William Chepman and former Rouen printer Andrew Myllar to import a printing press and set it up in Southgate, what is now called Cowgate, in Edinburgh. As well as halting the reliance on England and Europe, it also meant that religious books could be written in the Scottish style at home.

The king decreed that books of law, religion and Acts of Parliament should be printed and sold at a reasonable price, but that the export of manuscripts should be forbidden. Several of these original books are now housed in the National Library of Scotland in Edinburgh. The first specimens of the Scottish press were popular tales and ballads, but these were soon pushed aside for what was deemed more important work and it was another 20 years before more of such books were printed.

It could be argued that had James IV not been king of Scotland he may have gone on to accomplish great things. Perhaps he would have been an inventor, a scientist or even a doctor or surgeon. The interest was certainly there, and it is admirable that he used his energies constructively rather than destructively. He may well have gone to war, and he paid for this with his life, but much of his time was spent on improving the country and helping the people.

He took a country which for so long had been caught up with

warring clans and modernised it, taking it proudly into the sixteenth century. He planted the seeds for Scotland to grow into a prosperous country, leaving the Middle Ages firmly behind and instead looking forward.

Chapter 8

The Thistle And The Rose

James had made great efforts to make peace in Scotland. He was developing his country in many ways and he was by many accounts playing the part of a successful king. But he was never going to be completely successful until he married and produced at least one legitimate heir.

He had a nursery full of illegitimate children, but none of these could become king. Securing his position as king would help avoid rebels attempting to use one of his brothers or another close relative to overthrow him and place their own choice on the throne. He would only truly prove himself to be a successful king once he produced an heir, and a male one at that.

The negotiations for the marriage with Margaret had begun in 1496 at the time of Perkin Warbeck's stay in Scotland and were part of a peace deal. At the time Margaret was six and some historians doubt whether Henry Tudor was serious about the prospect of his daughter marrying the Scottish king. It would be years before she was of a marriageable age, and there were other contenders for her hand, Christian, son of King John of Denmark, being one of them.

Both Margaret's mother, and her grandmother, Lady Margaret Beaufort, were initially against the marriage. James was quite a bit older than Margaret – 16 years to be exact, and his reputation as a womaniser had reached as far as London. James, with his large brood of illegitimate children, was not the most eligible of bachelors.

In addition to this, the king's advisors were worried about what the marriage could mean for future generations, in particular the prospect of England ruling over Scotland. But Henry certainly never had any concerns that the marriage could lead to Scotland taking over England. When the suggestion was put to him at the time he is reported to have said,

> Supposing, which God forbid, that all my male progeny should become extinct, and the kingdom devolve by law to Margaret's heirs, will England be damaged thereby? For since it ever happens that the less becomes subservient to the greater the accession be that of Scotland to England, just as formerly happened to Normandy, which devolved upon our ancestors in the same manner, and was happily added to our kingdom by hereditary right as a rivulet to a fountain.

By 1502, probably because of a great desire to have peace between the two countries, Henry had decided that James was a good option for his daughter, and Scottish ambassadors were sent to London for the signing of the marriage treaty. This was a lengthy document. Henry Tudor was known to care deeply for his wife and children, and he took all steps to ensure she would be well looked after. The treaty stated that Margaret would receive dower lands of value enough to yield her an income of £2,000 per year. James would receive the revenues during his lifetime but was to pay for all that she needed – her residences, her horses, furniture, food, clothing, and all other expenses which she would be expected to incur as the queen of Scotland and the daughter of the king of England.

The document also stated that she should have plenty of servants, 24 of whom should be English, and she would receive 500 marks a year spending money.

As her dowry she brought James 30,000 golden nobles (equal to £10,000 sterling, £35,000 Scots) payable in three instalments – one third at the time of the wedding, one third a year later and one third two years later. This was a pretty small dowry and half the amount James had asked for in 1500. It was in fact smaller than the dowry that was offered to James III for Edward IV's daughter Cecilia in 1474 and smaller than the dowries received by James V in his two marriages.

Henry did, however, stick by his word and the first instalment was paid two days after the wedding in 1503, the second on 28 July 1504 and the third on 13 August 1505.

On 24 January 1502 the marriage treaty was signed, as was a treaty of permanent peace and friendship between the two countries. As was customary for royal weddings, in these times the initial ceremony was not attended by both parties. The promises which were made, while hard to compare to modern day wedding vows, being a prelude to the official wedding ceremony, were considered almost as legally binding as the marriage vows themselves.

At the betrothal, which took place at Richmond Palace, Patrick, the Earl of Bothwell, was proxy for James. Margaret, 12 at the time, was given the opportunity to refuse when the Archbishop of Glasgow asked her if she was content, without compulsion and of her own free will to go ahead. Her answer – Yes, if it pleases my lord father, the king, and my lady mother, the queen. They assured her it did.

There followed much celebration and festivities, including a banquet and a tournament, which Margaret greatly enjoyed. She was later to say that this was the best time of her life. She was surrounded by her family and friends (her brother Arthur died in the spring of that year, her mother died the following year) while being given the attention and pomp and ceremony of a queen.

When the following year the time came for Margaret to leave for Scotland Henry asked James how much he was going to pay her English servants on their long journey north. James managed to avoid the question, although he did agree to pay for her attendants once they were in Scotland.

On 27 June 1503 Margaret set off for Scotland. She would not have known if she would ever see London again, and along with her ladies, she would have had concerns about going into the unknown, and into the wild of Scotland at that. The king accompanied his daughter on the first stage of the journey, to Collyweston in

Northamptonshire, to Margaret Beaufort, Henry Tudor's mother and the person Margaret was named after.

John Young, Somerset Herald, was sent along for the journey to make an official record. He says she behaved with 'perfect propriety' on every occasion, playing the role given to her with remarkable poise and graciousness for such a young girl.

England was a much richer country than Scotland and the wealth was evident in the procession. Headed by the Earl of Surrey, with his countess as the princess's chaperone, the ladies rode on palfreys, or were drawn on litters when they approached and rode through important towns. As they passed through each town a sheriff and horsemen would ride ahead of her holding a white rod of office. The town officials would come out to meet her, and minstrels and other musicians would add to the entertainment.

One can imagine the excitement of the people looking to see the soon-to-be Scottish queen, daughter of their own King Henry. It was unlikely that most of them had even been part of anything like this before or would ever experience anything like this again.

The entourage reached Berwick at the end of July, the last English town before the border. As they were approaching Lamberton Kirk, the English party was met by Scottish emissaries sent by James, as well as the Archbishop of Glasgow accompanied by noblemen, knights and squires, all dressed formally for the occasion.

Stopping for a break, they were all given refreshments, quite a mean feat considering the numbers – approximately one thousand Scots and nearly twice as many English. Admittedly most of the English left for home at that point.

If the English were impressed by the generous nature of the Scots, they would soon think again. As they travelled through Scotland, they were regularly offered beer, supplied to them at a price by peasants looking to make a bit of money.

The group moved to Dunbar next, spending the night at a nunnery in Haddington. By 2 August they arrived at the Earl of Morton's castle at Dalkeith.

Officially the bride and groom were to meet at Edinburgh, but records tell us that James could not wait and met her at Dalkeith. This may seem very romantic and it was really but was also not that unusual in the sixteenth century.

At their first meeting Margaret was wearing a green velvet gown with a low-cut neck, which showed off her pearl necklace. James wore a jacket of red velvet with a gold lining. Margaret dropped to curtsey and James bowed low before kissing her on the cheek. He then kissed each of her ladies and greeted the Earl of Surrey and his wife.

James and Margaret then went to the side to speak, him a man of 29, her a young girl of 13, not much older than his eldest daughter. From there they went to the great hall for a meal, where James demonstrated perfect manners, insisting that Margaret be served first. After the meal and dancing had finished, they parted, providing Margaret's ladies with the opportunity to find out what she thought of him. They were impressed, considering him handsome, but Margaret was less forthcoming. 'His beard is too long' was her reply.

Next, they moved to the abbey at Newbattle where they spent four nights, the king visiting her regularly and always being the perfect gentleman. When it came to riding in to Edinburgh, and for the grand entrance, they rode in together, to the sound of pipers and minstrels, and to crowds of people waiting for the first glimpse of the new queen.

At the entrance to the town a big wooden gate with two towers had been erected. Someone stood at the entrance singing, while someone else approached her and presented her with the keys to the town. Margaret certainly received a warm welcome.

The official marriage ceremony was conducted at Holyrood Abbey on 8 August 1503, performed by the archbishops of York and Glasgow. As the bride and groom were distantly related (from John Beaufort) the letter from the pope confirming his permission for the marriage to take place was read out.

Immediately afterwards Margaret was anointed queen. From there James escorted his new wife to her chambers and then went to his own apartments to hold the Estate Royal for the day. When dinner was served in the evening again the king insisted that his new wife be served first. The room where they ate had recently been decorated, with the windows adorned with the Arms of Scotland and England, displaying the English rose and the Scottish thistle interlaced through a crown.

The Archbishop of Glasgow dined at the queen's table, alongside her highest-ranking ladies and some high-born Scottish ladies. The dinner was fit for a new queen – the first course consisted of 12 dishes. There was much fanfare, and the queen herself must have been exhausted. Leaving her friends and family and travelling all the way up to Scotland would have been tiring enough for a 13-year-old girl, never mind all the excitement of the past couple of days' events. Even during the time put aside for relaxation, she could not totally switch off and would have had to be on alert for visits from James.

In fact, in a letter written home to her father shortly after she arrived, Margaret wrote that she had no leisure time. Some historians have viewed this first letter home in a negative light, describing her as selfish and self-centred, but it was more likely that she was simply homesick and finding being in a foreign country tough. This was a 13-year-old girl after all, and while some of her ladies were to stay with her permanently, many left soon after the celebrations had ended.

Forty-one men were knighted by the king that week in honour of the new queen. The king was obviously in high spirits.

The king and queen continued to get to know each other and James would go to her apartments most nights to play cards with her and her ladies, playing the lute when she requested, and being entertained together by minstrels. During the day he took her hunting or hawking when he could.

Gradually James was able show her the country he loved. She was impressed with Stirling Castle, although she didn't find it a comfortable castle, and she was shocked to discover the royal nursery where James's illegitimate children were being brought up. James does appear to have had great affection for all his children and enjoyed seeing them. For Margaret, a 13-year-old girl, young and innocent, this was a bit too much to contend with and the decision was soon made to have the children moved when Margaret was at Stirling. However, we have no knowledge of what her reaction was when another of James's children, the Lady Margaret, was moved to live in Edinburgh Castle, just along from the queen's home at Holyrood.

James soon told Margaret the story behind his iron belt. Margaret listened to the story but could not understand his guilt. In her eyes the noblemen were the guilty ones and he had done nothing wrong.

There was one bit of bad news in the new year of 1504 when the king's younger brother James, Duke of Ross, and Archbishop of St Andrews, died at the age of 27. James may have often been suspicious of him, largely due to his father's actions and favouritism towards the younger James, but James appears to have treated him well and treated him fairly once he became king. He would have mourned his death, particularly as both his brothers were now dead, his youngest brother John, Earl of Marr, having died early the previous year.

In March 1504 the queen was formally crowned when the Scottish Parliament met. They confirmed her dower rights and a copy of this document was sent to her father in London. Henry then made the payment of her wedding dower that was now due and reimbursed James for the expenses incurred by the wedding party in Scotland. Her father appeared to be happy with things, and so did Margaret. In a letter to her brother, the future Henry VIII, she wrote, 'We lack nothing'.

In the summer of 1504 Margaret remained at Stirling Castle while James travelled to Dumfries to attend the ayre. She spent time riding and taking part in archery and began to make her mark on the royal castle, supervising changes being made to the castle.

Royal records show us that James showered his new bride with gifts. But there were also records of other expensive gifts being given to 'L of A'. Margaret would have heard rumours about James's other women and certainly the royal nursery was concrete evidence that there had been others, but we do not know how she reacted or what her thoughts were on her husband's mistresses.

Scotland was a very different country from England and Margaret was used to a very high standard of living which the money from her dower lands failed to cover. James also had to pay for her pension and the salaries of her attendants. As well as this, there was the cost of maintaining her stables, furniture and clothing. Clothing alone amounted to one thousand pounds a year.

The main reason for getting married was to have children and produce heirs, and on 21 February 1507 the royal couple welcomed a baby boy into the world. One can imagine the reaction – from James, the proud father, delighted that he had produced a male heir, from Margaret, the mother, happy that she had fulfilled her duty and so could relax a bit, but also from the people throughout the land, peasants and nobility. It had been many years since there had been a royal birth, and good news like this was always good for a country's morale.

When he was two days old the baby James, after his father and grandfather before him, was baptised in a glorious ceremony. Messengers were sent to various parts of Scotland to let the people know, as well as to Henry VII in London.

There was much excitement and celebration, but this was short-lived as the queen fell critically ill. James was distraught but, rather than stay by her side to support her, he set off on foot to the shrine of St Ninian to pray for her health. This was an eight-day journey so not an easy option. But all throughout his life he viewed any kind of misfortune that he suffered as God punishing him for the part he played in his father's death, and now was no exception. By the time he arrived back her health had improved, and she was expected to survive. James told her the story that her health had taken a positive turn at the exact moment he had bent down to pray.

By July he had persuaded her that they should personally say thanks to St Ninian for her recovery and so they rode with her ladies in waiting, servants, minstrels and entertainers to the shrine. The sight was quite different from when James had made the trip earlier in the year, and it was reported that they required 17 horses to carry all of the queen's bags, and four to carry the king's.

But, sadly, the little prince died in 1508 at the age of 12 months. The queen was already expecting another baby, but this baby, a girl, died soon after birth. Another baby boy, Arthur, was born in 1509 but like his brother and sister before him he died, this time at nine months.

In the spring of 1511 Margaret made another pilgrimage, perhaps in the hope of producing a healthy child who would live. This one was to another one of James's favourites – St Duthac. The following year Margaret gave birth to another boy on 10 April. By this point they must have been emotionally exhausted from losing so many children. And the five years of near constant pregnancy and childbirth would have had its toll on Margaret. But this baby was to live past infanthood, and would in time become King James V.

The queen again gave birth in November 1512, but the baby girl died immediately. Meanwhile the attention of the king and queen was now being taken up with other problems. Despite having signed a peace treaty a mere ten years previously, relationships were not going well between England and Scotland. And the marriage, which was very much part of the peace deal, and which was to ensure enduring peace, was doing nothing to help things. They were already on the road to Flodden.

Chapter 9

European Unions

It is very easy to criticise James IV for being the cause of his own downfall – both in his death and how he has been portrayed in history. And many have done this. The king who did so much for Scotland, and who cared deeply for his people and his country, was cut down in the prime of his life, in what many have described as an act of folly. The picture painted is one of James as the French king's whipping boy, willing to go to war with England because Louis had asked, leading to his unnecessary death and the minority rule of the new infant king.

But the story is a bit more complicated than that. The war with England did not suddenly materialise in 1513. It had been a slow-burning fire that finally went up in flames after several attempts to extinguish it.

Certainly, James appears to have made a good job of avoiding war for so long. Following Henry VII's death in April 1509 the correspondence between James and the new King Henry VIII was amiable, with each viewing the other as their brother.

When in 1504 his uncle, King John of Denmark, made a request for two well-armed, equipped ships, to be sent to help deal with problems he was having with the Swedish people, James politely refused, while at the same time advising John to go easy on them. Writing to the Swedes he encouraged them to make peace but warned that if his uncle was put in danger he would get involved.

Over the next couple of years, as King John dealt with problems at home, he made several requests to King James for help. But rather than send men and ships James was keener on helping negotiate a peace deal. In 1507 he sent Robert Forman, Dean of Glasgow, to investigate and to encourage peace between King John and the Swedish people, and to mediate between the people of Lübeck and Denmark. The dispute between Lübeck and Denmark had been going on for some time and they were now supporting the Swedish people in their rebellion against Denmark.

As the situation for King John improved and then worsened, he made several appeals to James to send help. James either avoided the question or suggested an alternative, more peaceful way of quelling the rebellion.

Meanwhile King Louis XII was also looking for help. In 1507 the French king requested from James 4,000 well-trained foot soldiers to help in the defence of the Duchy of Milan. Louis insisted that the men should be sent, even if the threat was not to materialise, as a token that the Auld Alliance was still in force. He did not in the end need them but reiterated to James to have them ready just in case he did. James, for his part, had become very good at avoiding the question. While James replied asking Louis to regard him as a kinsman and brother he could rely on, he also asked how many soldiers were required, a question Louis had already answered.

Relationships between England and Scotland were very shaky. In 1508 the Scottish Warden of the Marches, Sir Robert Kerr, had been murdered by, 'The Bastard John Heron', brother of Sir William Heron of Ford Castle in Northumberland. This had happened during a truce between England and Scotland and James expected Henry to punish Heron and his accomplices. 'The Bastard Heron' managed to avoid punishment but James did not let go of this grudge and he did eventually get his revenge on the family in 1513.

Henry needed to know where he stood with James. He was well aware that the Scottish king's allegiances were divided. The mood in the Scottish court favoured renewing the Auld Alliance with France. James was undecided as Thomas Wolsey found in 1508 when he was sent to Scotland to try to gauge the situation. While before Wolsey's arrival he had been edging towards renewing the Auld Alliance, he now gave Henry reassurance that as long as he kept acting like a good father, he would remain loyal to him.

King Louis in France was also getting a bit concerned. Under the pretence that he was consulting James about the marriage of the future Francis I of France to Princess Claude of France, Bernard Stewart, Lord of Aubigny, arrived in Scotland in May 1508. He had in fact been sent by King Louis to sound James out on the renewal of the Auld Alliance. James welcomed him and made him a member of the Order of St Michael, but he died in Scotland that summer, still waiting on the answer.

Shortly after Aubigny's death James did indeed send Gavin Dunbar, archdeacon of St Andrews and clerk register, to France on the *Treasurer*, bearing messages of goodwill and promises that the treaty of 1492 would be renewed, but with no concrete plans to put these promises into action.

On its return journey the *Treasurer* hit trouble and was wrecked on the east coast of England. The travellers were taken to be interviewed by King Henry, who was possibly looking to gain information on the nature of their journey, but they were soon released.

In the first few years of the sixteenth century there was plenty of movement on the dance floor of European politics. In December 1508 the League of Cambrai was formed, consisting of the Holy Roman Emperor Maximilian, Ferdinand of Aragon and Louis XII of France. Pope Julius joined a few months later.

The league was set up to fight against the over-mighty republic of Venice and return towns and lands to the countries the republic had seized them from. Successful in its mission, by 1510 it had been disbanded and the pope, whose working relationship with France had broken down, was now working with Venice against France, in what was to become known as the Holy League.

A war between the pope and France now looked likely. James, keen to play the part of peacemaker, sent Andrew Forman to attempt reconciliation. But he also had an ulterior motive. Thoughts of a crusade to the Holy Land were never far from his mind and

Forman was also to get details on how Louis would assist him in making this journey, how many guns, ships and troops he would provide him with, and for how long, and how much money he was prepared to give for this purpose. He also wanted to know whether Alexandria or Constantinople should be priority.

Forman's journey was unsuccessful on both accounts. Louis appears to have had no intention of assisting James in a crusade, and the fall-out with the pope had only just begun. Pope Julius had moved on and had been negotiating with the ambassadors of England, Spain and Venice, an agreement for a new alliance – the Holy League.

The previous year Henry VII had died, replaced by his son Henry VIII. Within six months, in the presence of nobles and prelates, James had sworn on the gospels to observe every article in the Treaty of Perpetual Peace. So, France, which had only a few years previously been surrounded by friends, was now out on its own and in need of allies like Scotland. Very quickly Louis sent an envoy to Scotland, with the request that Scotland stay faithful to France and for James not to join the Holy League, while at the same time stressing that he should not break with England.

Around the same time Maximilian appealed to James to join with him and Louis to help avert war. He also dangled the bait that this would help make possible James's dream of a crusade.

James was doing his best to stay neutral. In 1512 he again sent Forman to Rome to try to make peace between the pope and Louis. He suggested that if the pope would abandon the Holy League, Louis would give up Bologna and Ferrara. But Julius was sold in his belief that Louis was trying to destroy the church and he urged James to join him in the Holy League. Henry meanwhile was now in partnership with Ferdinand of Spain, and they were planning a joint invasion of France.

Forman returned to Scotland with instruction from Louis to encourage James to keep peace with Henry, as a way of laying down foundations for a crusade, while at the same time stressing that that time was not now. He promised that a year after peace was established, he would provide him with plenty of funds, men, equipment and ships, but on condition that James refuse to join the Holy League, and pressurise the pope into holding his general council somewhere neutral.

One can't help wonder what was going through James's mind when he kept asking for direct help in order to pursue a crusade, each time being fobbed off with vague promises. Today he comes across as a bit gullible in this respect but judging in hindsight is easy to do.

The Auld Alliance was finally renewed in March 1512. James wrote to the pope complaining of his treatment of Louis, and in reply to Ferdinand's request that he join the Holy League he attempted to convince Ferdinand to make peace with Louis and the pope.

France was becoming more and more alienated. Spain, Switzerland and Venice were now France's enemies. Maximilian was about to join the Holy League, increasing the number on the opposite side from France, and England was making plans to invade France. The first draft of the new treaty was taken to France in early 1512 and it couldn't have come at a better time.

In April 1512 Louis sent Robert Cockburn, Bishop of Ross, as an envoy from France, with instructions to be relayed to James. Cockburn was chaplain to Louis and acted as a go-between for France and Scotland on several occasions, until his death in 1526.

He was to ask James to send an ambassador to France, with a message that, should Henry declare war with Louis, on the pretext of helping Ferdinand of Spain, James would make war on him, in support of Louis.

Louis was continuing to play James, but James for his part, although he had renewed the Auld Alliance, was still not keen to go to war with England. He wrote back to Louis highlighting the fact that he was concerned that a war with Henry might have a negative impact on his claim to the English throne, should Henry VIII die childless. As he was married to Henry's sister, he or his descendants would have a valid claim. He asked for Louis's support on this matter should he need it but also made certain requests of Louis.

James stated that he would prefer that a war with England was a sea war only. He also wanted money, provisions and troops from Louis. Louis, quick to reply, encouraged him to fight both on sea and land, and apologised for the fact that his commitments fighting in Italy meant that he could not provide him with more assistance.

Louis was determined to hold on to James as a friend, fobbing him off when James asked directly for help, but letting him think that should matters come to a head he would be there for him. It may now look as if James was a bit of a fool and had become a French puppet, but James was not making silly errors of judgement. Decisions were discussed with the General Council and advice was sought from some very knowledgeable statesmen.

Meanwhile Henry was also looking for reassurance from James, and he sent ambassadors to the Scottish court in order to get James's support in the coming war but failing that his neutrality. But his request of – if you don't fight with us, at least don't fight against us – was met with non-commitment from James.

June 1512 saw the Scottish court receive another visitor when de la Motte arrived in Scotland with a copy of the new treaty, signed by Louis the previous month, but with the redundant clauses deleted. The fifth clause was amended to a simple declaration that neither party would enter into a truce with England without the other's consent. As always Louis's loyalty was conveyed.

De la Motte, on his return journey, sailed in a ship belonging to William Brownhill, and was escorted by the ships of Robert Barton and David Falconer. By August word had reached James that Brownhill's ship had been shot down by the English and that the remaining ships had been forced to head for Denmark. A supplicate treaty was then duly sent.

James had already tried to get Denmark to help and had sent an envoy to King John, requesting that Denmark help France and Scotland, should either one be attacked by England. John, not keen to get involved as he had enough of his own troubles at home, advised James to keep the truce with Henry.

Children can be frustrating at times. They have a tendency to annoy their siblings or classmates for the fun of it, getting much enjoyment out of troublemaking. And so it was the case also with the three monarchs – Louis, Henry and James. Each of them, at some point, took great enjoyment in playing games with one of the others. James was certainly no innocent as the Perkin Warbeck episode proved. And in the final years before Flodden it was Louis who was having fun, this time by harbouring the Yorkist Richard de la Pole.

De la Pole, the last remaining member of the House of York and the son of John de la Pole, Duke of Suffolk, and Elizabeth of York, was considered a threat by King Henry as he could possibly either be a contender for the crown or be used as a pawn by those wanting to get rid of the Tudors. Louis recognised him as King Richard IV, the news of which would have brought back memories of James's recognition of Perkin Warbeck as Richard, Duke of York. With relationships between France and Scotland not at their best this set only to worsen things.

Henry, for his part, continued to frustrate his sister and brother-in-law by refusing to give Margaret the remaining part of her legacy owed to her from her brother's death. She had made repeated requests, both by letter and in person when diplomats had arrived in Scotland to speak with her. Not only was withholding of funds insulting, but the money was needed.

Tensions were heightening and by August 1512 the Earl of Surrey was sent north with forces. He got as far as Yorkshire where he stayed for a month, waiting for news that the Scots had crossed the border. His wait was in vain and by the middle of October men and supplies started to be sent back to London.

So why didn't James attack at this time? The reason had a lot to do with a deadlock with France. James had requested from Louis the removal of a clause and this was still being finalised.

Over the next few months James tried in vain to bring peace in Europe, acting as a mediator between the pope and Louis but all was in vain. In February Pope Julius, while on his deathbed, issued letters threatening James with excommunication. When the pope died, and he was replaced by Leo X James sent Andrew Forman to Europe to request that the new pope not confirm the sentence. The response was negative. The pope accused James of dividing

Christendom, ordering him to keep the peace with Henry and promising him that if he did invade England he would be excommunicated.

But this letter came too late. In May 1513 a practical offer finally came from Louis, when he promised James that he would equip the Scottish fleet, send seven galleys commanded by one of his most experienced admirals, and would send 50,000 francs (about £22,500).

For this he asked of James that he should invade England as soon as Henry had left for France, at the same time sending some of the Scottish navy to France, ideally with some ships from Denmark. He also promised that, once the war was over, he would assist James in achieving his ambition of going to the Holy Land for a crusade. Denmark was a lost cause. King John had recently died, and the new king had other priorities. But James was by now prepared to make a move on his own.

As requested, in July, James sent six ships, including the *Great Michael*, to France, and sent a message to Henry that he should desist from further invasion and destruction of Louis, or he would have no choice but to go to war with him.

In early 1513 the European chess pieces began to move, resulting in the chessboard looking quite different. In March the Venetians withdrew from the Holy League, as they were not prepared to work with the Emperor Maximilian. Instead they made a treaty with France. Then Ferdinand of Spain concluded a one-year truce with Louis, while leading the Holy League to believe that he was still working with them. But James's days of diplomacy were over and only days of war lay ahead.

There are several myths and legends surrounding Flodden and one of the first involves a warning from a mysterious figure. At the start of August the king and queen were in Linlithgow. Here, as the story goes, a stranger approached the king while he was sitting in the Church of St Michael. Described as having very blonde hair, a great staff and a long blue robe, the man spoke to the king and gave him two pieces of advice. Claiming that the warning had come from his mother, he told the king that he should not go to war, for the result would not be a good one. He also warned the king not to get involved with women.

The story, although told as if the figure was an apparition, comes from more than one source, and it is likely that the figure was real and was initiated by someone in the court who did not want a war with England to happen.

But the appeal was useless whatever the motives. James had already made one last half-hearted appeal to Henry when he wrote to him in May at the suggestion of Louis. In the letter he had offered to enter into a truce arranged by the kings of France and Aragon if Henry would do the same.

Nothing came of the plea and within weeks it was too late. At the end of June Henry left England for France. The time for action, as agreed with Louis, had come, and war between Scotland and England was now imminent.

Louis's wife, Anne of Brittany, had also stepped in and in May of that year de la Motte had returned from France with a letter and a turquoise ring from the queen. Referring to James as her knight, she requested that he step three feet onto English ground and strike one blow. Anne, or probably her husband Louis, was playing on the fact that James was known for liking the ladies.

On 25 July, as per James's promise to Louis, the Scottish fleet, along with several other ships, sailed out into the Forth, under the command of the king's cousin, James Hamilton, Earl of Arran.

In England Henry had left the queen to act as regent in his absence, with the Earl of Surrey to be Lieutenant in the north. While several of his advisors did not believe that James would actually invade, Henry was not so sure and was taking no risks. Surrey left for the north towards the end of July and on 1 August he arrived at Pontefract.

On 8 August James made one final pilgrimage to St Duthac. Within the week the Lyon King-of-Arms had been sent to the English camp with an ultimatum that he should not invade France. The ultimatum was rebuked, and war had now begun.

Chapter 10

Flodden

Margaret Tudor was now in the position where her husband was at war with her brother, her adopted homeland fighting with her native land. One wonders the emotions which she would have gone through, particularly as her son and only heir to the throne was still a baby. But we do know that Margaret was firmly behind James's actions and supported him in the belief that going to war was the only solution to the ongoing crisis.

Records tell us that in Edinburgh on 18 August the men in charge of the guns were paid 14 days' wages at a shilling a day for service in Scotland, and a further eight days payment for services in England at the higher rate of 16p a day. With 17 large guns James was assembling one of the largest armies to invade England.

Following the Medieval code of chivalry James sent notice to the English one month before he planned to attack, allowing them time to gather an army and retrieve the banner of St Cuthbert from Durham Cathedral, a banner which had been carried into victory by the English in 1138 and 1341. Henry had given the job of defending the north to Thomas Howard, Earl of Surrey, a 70-year-old man at the time of Flodden, but a capable and experienced leader in battle.

Surrey had expected to lead the invasion of France, so was primed for battle. Along with his sons Thomas and Edmund he made his way north to Northumberland.

Norham Castle was James's initial target, which sat just south of the river Tweed, and was Bishop Ruthal's great stronghold. Ruthal was one of Henry VIII's leading councillors and had gone to France with Henry but was sent back to England when war with Scotland became imminent.

Between 19 and 22 August the Scots moved over the Lammermuir Hills to Ellem, and over the course of five days they had captured Norham Castle. Ruthal, at this time Bishop of Durham, wrote to Wolsey in London that he would never forget, nor recover, from the grief of losing the castle.

A good start had been made and James's intentions were to continue further into England. On 29 August his treasurer was sent back to Edinburgh for more ammunition, oxen and wheels for the gun carriages.

The next successes were the castles of Ford and Etal, which were taken at the start of September. Ford Castle is only six miles from the border and was owned by Lord Heron, at that time a prisoner in Scotland. The story goes that Elizabeth, Lady Heron, entertained James, with his son, the Archbishop of St Andrews enjoying the company of her daughter.

Lady Heron made every effort to persuade the Scottish king to spare the castle. James agreed on condition that two of his knights, Lord Johnstone and Alexander Hume, be freed before midday on 5 September. The exchange was agreed with the Earl of Surrey, but Lady Heron's bargaining was in vain as the castle was burnt anyway.

James has been criticised for his dalliance at Ford Castle. He wasted time here, which gave the English more time to prepare. Having invaded England and captured one castle, one would have expected him to have moved forward and attacked the larger castles of the north, instead of what appears to be wasted time at Ford Castle.

By early September the Scots had taken up a strong position on Flodden Hill. There had been some desertions – these often were due to soldiers not receiving payment, but also, in this case, the first couple of weeks had gone so well that some thought the battle had already been won.

But with at least 12 earls and 20 lords of parliament with him he must have still felt confident. On Thursday 8 September Surrey and his men moved north past where the Scots were, settling close to the fords of Twizel and Herton on the River Till. This would have been a good time for the Scots to attack the English, but for whatever reason they did not, allowing Surrey's army time to move south and west across the Till at Twizel and Herton, and had soon reached the foot of Branxton Hill. As this was a few miles north of the Scots it blocked any retreat by the Scots to Scotland, and also meant that their guns were facing the wrong way, forcing them to move quickly across the two miles of dividing high ground to the top of Branxton Hill before the English got there.

The battle began at 4pm and, despite the Scottish army being of similar size to the English (reports were that the Scots had more than 30,000, the English approximately 26,000), things did not go well for the Scots. The rough, muddy ground of Branxton Hill was unsuitable for a rapid tight formation of the pikemen and the marshy ground, made worse by the poor weather, did not help the situation.

The English weapons were superior to the Scots'. Their pikes stood no chance against the English brown bill, an eight-foot spear axe with various hooks and sharp ends in which to hurt and pierce the enemy.

Many of the English archers came from Lancashire and Cheshire. When Sir Richard Assheton rebuilt his parish church – St Leonard's in Middleton, near Manchester, he included what is known as the Flodden Window, depicting and naming the local archers and their priest, who had fought at Flodden.

One of biggest criticisms of James was that he led his army from the front, putting him at most risk of being killed. The Scots also placed their officers in the front line in the old medieval style, while the English followed the Renaissance style of having the generals at the back. What ensued was chaos. There were so many casualties on the Scottish side that it wasn't until after the battle had ended that the king's body was found on the field, pierced by an arrow. The loss of so many Scottish officers meant that there had been no one to organise a retreat.

Bishop Ruthal, who had only days earlier lost his castle to James, wrote to Wolsey that the Scottish king had fallen near his banner, and died. He also paid tribute to the courage and strength of the Scots. This was the last time a Scottish king would die on the battlefield.

The English meanwhile took no prisoners, but 'slew and stripped' the king, bishops, nobles and lords, leaving them naked on the field.

The English lost approximately one thousand five hundred men according to English accounts at the time, other later estimates go up to four thousand. The Scots lost about ten thousand – all within just two and a half hours. It would be another four hundred years before a rate of slaughter anything like this was seen, during World War One.

Alongside the king the dead included his son the Archbishop of St Andrews, two bishops, two abbots, nine earls and 15 lords. They had also lost all of their artillery. It was said that there was barely a family in Scotland that wasn't impacted by the deaths at Flodden. With the heads and heirs of most of the landed family in Scotland now lost it is understandable that some historians say Scotland never recovered. Of the three earls who did survive the battle, one lost a brother, the other two lost sons. A similar story is told of the other survivors. In contrast Surrey knighted 45 English soldiers after the battle.

William Elphinstone, Bishop of Aberdeen, had long pleaded for his country to make peace with England and not to go to war. When he heard the result of the battle his biographer tells us that he was overwhelmed with grief, fell into a depression for the rest of his life and never laughed again.

By the following day the first rumours of the defeat had arrived back at Edinburgh. Immediately the burgh council gathered and issued a proclamation, requesting that what men there were left in the capital were to get ready to defend their city. Women were to refrain from showing public grief and instead were to focus on going to church to pray for the king and all those who had died, and to carry on as normal:

We do yow to witt, Forsamekill as thair is ane greit rumour now laitlie rysin within this toun tuiching our Souerane Lord and his army, of the quhilk we understand thair is cumin na veritie as yit, thairfore we charge straitlie and commandis in our said Souerane Lord the Kingis name, and the presedentis for the provest and baillies within this burgh, that all maner of personis nychtbouris within the samyn haue reddye thair fensabill geir and wapponis for weir, and compeir thariwith to the said presidentis at jowyng of the commoun bell, for the keiping and defens of the toun aganis thame that wald invalid the samyn.

And als charigis that all wemen, and specialie vageboundis, that thai pas to thair labouris and be nocht sene vpoun the gait clamorand and cryand, vnder the pane of banesing of the personis but fauouris, and that the vther wemen of gude pas to the kirk and pray quhane tyme requiris for our Souerane Lord and his armye and nychtbouris being thairat, and hald thame at thair previe labouris of the gait within thair houssis as efferis.

This result had certainly not been foreseen. The English did not have a vastly larger army, and the Earl of Surrey was aged 70 at the time of the battle, anything but a young man, but at the same time an experienced and capable military man. For days they had gone without beer or ale to drink. Having already captured three castles, the Scots would have been feeling confident.

But in the centuries following the battle James has been much criticised for showing poor leadership and coordination. When the battle began he positioned himself so that he was most exposed to attack and least able to control his troops. Instead of working together, the units worked separately, creating one unorganised shambles.

Poor weather conditions made the ground incompatible with successful combat. Or certainly they could have chosen a better place to fight. More planning of where they were going to fight and some strategic thinking beforehand would have benefited them greatly.

Another criticism has been the lack of military skill. Soldiers were not trained and had no experience of war. The naval battle fared no better. The fleet arrived a month late, as Arran had stopped to plunder Carrickfergus.

The king's body was not discovered until the following day, identified by Thomas, Lord Dacre, who knew the king well and had gone hawking with him in the past. It was taken to Berwick where again it was identified by Sir John Forman, the king's sergeant-porter and a member of the king's council, Sir William Scott.

From there it was moved south to the Carthusian monastery at Sheen, at that time seven miles north of London. There they were hit with the problem of what to do with it. As James had been excommunicated before he died, Henry had to write to the pope requesting that he write to the Bishop of London to allow him to have the body carried to London and buried with royal honours at St Paul's Cathedral. In November Leo replied that he presumed that James has sought repentance for his sins before he died and so he could be buried with funeral honours.

However, the death of James IV was not accepted by all, and many believed that a mistake had been made and that he was alive and well.

For a long time there were rumours in the Borders that James had not died, and the Catholic priest and historian Bishop Lesley wrote in 1568 that the body recovered was not that of the king but belonged to another Scottish lord. Backing up his story, he wrote that the king left the battlefield to go on pilgrimage to Jerusalem and never returned to Scotland.

George Buchanan claimed that as many other Scots in the battle wore the same coat as the king, it was easy to get them mixed up and that Alexander, first Lord Elphinstone, had in fact been mistaken for him. This ignores the fact that he was found semi-naked and that he had been identified by men who knew him.

But small details have never got in the way of a good story and Buchanan repeats the story that James had been seen by eye witnesses re-crossing the Tweed and had been killed there. So, in other words the king was dead but the body the English now had was not his.

Pitscottie has a similar story to tell, asserting that James, while not killed at the battle, was killed soon after. About ten years after Flodden a man convicted of murder offered to show the Duke of Albany where the late king was buried, in exchange for his life. As proof he promised that with the body would be the king's iron belt. Albany did not pay any attention to him and so the story ends.

Another story has him being taken from the battlefield by four mysterious horsemen and supernatural figures, determined that the English would not get their hands on his body. And in the eighteenth century when Hume Castle, near Kelso, was being cleared it was said that the skeleton of a man wearing an iron belt was found, although no evidence survives.

There have been various other stories over the years, all along the same lines – that the king had survived the battle and he had either disappeared off to Jerusalem or had been killed shortly after the battle and was buried somewhere in the Borders, as opposed to his body being in the hands of the English.

Why were there so many rumours surrounding his death? It is likely that this is because he was so well thought of by the people that they didn't want to accept it. But, also, the sad fate of Flodden was so unbelievable to many – that the king had died, and that what should have been a victory was in fact a catastrophic loss. In the same way hundreds of years later Elvis Presley was adored and when he died people found it hard to believe that he was now gone forever, Scots in the sixteenth century found it hard to believe that their charismatic, adored king was gone forever. And just like in modern day times, people will ignore the most obvious of evidence in favour of their own version.

Before he had left for war James had made arrangements should he not return. He had appointed his wife Margaret as regent for their infant son James, who was not quite 17 months old.

Louis, for his part, viewed the defeat as a disappointment, but was not overly affected by it. The *Great Michael*, once Scotland's pride and joy, was sold to France for 40,000 francs, and soon faded from the records.

France had sent considerable money, arms and troops to help Scotland but sadly they had arrived too late. Soon after the battle Louis granted new privileges to Scotsmen resident in France. From now on they would be considered equal to Frenchmen resident in Scotland and would no longer have to apply for letters of naturalisation in order to dispose of their goods.

Louis also ensured that Andrew Forman, Bishop of Moray, was rewarded. It was to Forman he gave credit for persuading James to go to war. After much persuasion and reported force on the part of Louis, Bourge eventually accepted Forman as archbishop. Forman, incidentally, was the brother of Adam Forman, standard bearer to the king at Flodden, and John, the king's sergeant-porter who was captured at the battle.

As for the great division within Europe, matters very rapidly changed. Although Arran returned from France with a request that the alliance be reconfirmed, France was no longer the child at the party standing away from the crowd with no friends. In October Louis made peace with the pope. A few weeks later he opened up negotiations with Ferdinand, and the following year England and France officially made peace, securing this with a marriage treaty between the elderly King Louis (Anne of Brittany died just a few months after Flodden) and the young Princess Mary, youngest sister of King Henry VIII. But Louis himself did not survive long and died on 1 January 1515.

It is perhaps not too surprising that when the English and French were negotiating a peace treaty the Scots were included. They were given three months to apply to be included, but in the meantime if they made any raids into England this offer would be withdrawn. The Scots accepted, they refrained from raiding England, and on 24 August 1514 the council informed Louis and his ambassadors that Scotland would adhere to the treaty.

Surrey was rewarded for his achievement and on 1 February 1514 he was created Duke of Norfolk, with his son Thomas taking the title of Earl of Surrey. Both were given lands and annuities.

Their family coat of arms was also adapted, to include a picture of the lion of Scotland pierced through the mouth with an arrow.

One could wonder what would have happened had things been different and James had won the battle. But an ultimate victory really was unlikely. If the Scots had won Flodden, at Nottingham Sir Thomas Lovell was waiting with 15,000 men, ready to move in to assist Surrey.

And if perhaps the Scots had beaten Lovell's men it is unlikely that Henry would have ever accepted defeat from the Scots. An invasion of Scotland would have been made and the bloodshed would have continued.

Flodden had been a disaster, and while for the English it had no long-lasting impact, for the Scots it would be forever remembered in the words of this ballad – 'Flowers of the Forest' – about the grief of the families at the loss of their men.

I've heard the lilting, at the yowe-milking,
Lasses a-lilting before dawn o' day;
But now they are moaning on ilka green loaning;
'The Flowers of the Forest are a' wede away'.
As buchts, in the morning, nae blythe lads are scorning;
The lasses are lonely and dowie and wae.
Nae daffin', nae gabbin', but sighing and sobbing,
Ilk ane lifts her leglen, and hies her away.
In hairst, at the shearing, nae youths now are jeering,
The Bandsters are lyart, and runkled and grey.
At fair or at preaching, nae wooing, nae fleeching,
The Flowers of the Forest are a' wede away.
At e'en, in the gloaming, nae swankies are roaming,
'Bout stacks wi' the lasses at bogle to play.
But ilk ane sits drearie, lamenting her dearie,
The Flowers of the Forest are a' wede away.
Dule and wae for the order sent our lads to the Border;
The English, for ance, by guile wan the day:
The Flowers of the Forest, that foucht aye the foremost,
The prime o' our land are cauld in the clay.

We'll hae nae mair lilting, at the yowe-milking,
Women and bairns are dowie and wae.
Sighing and moaning, on ilka green loaning,
The Flowers of the Forest are all wede away.

Chapter 11

Aftermath

The king was dead, his heir was barely 17 months old, and the queen – an English woman – had been named as regent until such time as she remarried. She was also two months' pregnant with James's child.

Following the late king's wishes Parliament met at Stirling and confirmed Margaret as regent. It is likely that many were not happy about this arrangement. They had, after all, been defeated by the English, so to be ruled by one, and a woman at that, was obviously going to cause friction. Certainly, it didn't take long for them to look elsewhere – this time to another foreigner.

John Stewart, Duke of Albany, had been born and brought up in France, his father, Alexander Stewart, Duke of Albany, and brother to the late James III, having fled to France in 1479, where he married a French woman and remained.

But Margaret showed strength and may well have been a strong and successful regent, that is if she hadn't remarried so quickly and with such poor judgement. Scotland's history had always been dogged by rival families, competing with the others to gain favour with the king. The Douglases were one such family.

Margaret married Archibald Douglas, 6th Earl of Angus, on 6 August 1514, less than a year after her husband's death, and less than four months after the birth of her son Alexander, Duke of Ross. What was she thinking? Had they managed to convince her that she could maintain her role as regent, and that despite breaking the terms of her regency, she would be stronger with Douglas support? One does wonder.

If this was the case she would soon be proved wrong. The Privy Council met the following month and, as predicted, withdrew her rights to the regency and to supervision rights of her sons. Margaret quickly moved to Stirling Castle with her children, defying the Privy Council. But by May the following year Albany had arrived in Scotland, having accepted the request by the Scots to replace Margaret as regent. He was installed as regent in July, with taking custody of the two young princes being one of his top priorities.

There wasn't much point in Margaret fighting this and in August she surrendered and moved to Edinburgh without her sons. By now she was pregnant by Angus and the prospects for her in Scotland were looking increasingly glum. For some time now her brother Henry had been urging her to move back to England. She had always refused, but having lost her position as regent, as well as her sons, and with a baby on the way, she finally relented. She was granted permission to leave Edinburgh for Linlithgow and from there she escaped over the border, where she was received by Lord Dacre, her brother's Warden of the Marshes, and taken to Harbottle Castle in Northumberland where, in October of that year, she gave birth to a daughter, Lady Margaret Douglas, the future Countess of Lennox and mother of Henry Stuart, Lord Darnley, who would go on to marry another one of Margaret's grandchildren, Mary Queen of Scots.

Soon after arriving in England Margaret learned of the death of her younger son Alexander. Dacre tried to use this information to his advantage by suggesting that Albany was responsible, but Margaret was not that gullible. She knew that if Albany had wanted to kill one her sons in order to get closer to the crown James would have been the most obvious target.

Like her granddaughter, Mary Queen of Scots, Margaret Tudor did not have much success in marriage. Soon after arriving in England Angus made the decision to return to Scotland to make peace with Albany, leaving Margaret in England. This did not impress Margaret in the slightest, and it impressed her brother even less. On hearing that his sister and her newly born child had been abandoned by her husband he is reported to have said, 'Done like a Scot'. Admittedly it was a pretty bad thing to have done, but from Angus's point of view all his land, wealth and power were in Scotland.

Henry was dutiful to his sister, receiving her well and making sure she was adequately looked after, housing her in the ancient residence of Scottish kings in London, Scotland Yard. There she remained until a year later a treaty of reconciliation was signed by Albany, Henry and Cardinal Wolsey and Margaret returned to Scotland, where she was given limited access to her son.

Margaret and Angus did temporarily reconcile, until she discovered that he had been living with an old lover. Margaret had had enough and they parted ways, with Margaret eventually receiving an annulment from the pope in 1527. Her third marriage to Henry Stewart, later created Lord Methven, was also a poor marriage, although her son James V refused to allow her to divorce, and she spent the rest of her life complaining of poverty to her brother.

But it was not all doom and gloom for Margaret. Access to her son began to increase and her relationship with Albany improved (when the often-absent regent was in the country) and the two worked together at times. She spent the rest of her life in Scotland, following her son, the king, around. While she would often complain about this to Henry – she had little money of her own so financially she had to go with the court – it did mean that she was able to develop a relationship with her son, which different circumstances would not have allowed. She died in Methven Castle in Perthshire on 18 October 1541, just 14 months before her son was killed, having lived to see him grow up and marry Marie de Guise.

How a monarch is remembered is largely down to propaganda published after their death. Queen Mary, nicknamed Bloody Mary, has been portrayed mostly negatively, largely due to strong Catholic beliefs she held, which were at odds with the Protestant beliefs of Elizabethan times. So how was King James IV, a king who was both amiable and active as a king but who led his country into disaster, remembered?

George Buchanan was barely seven at the time of Flodden, but today provides one of the leading historical accounts of King James IV. The Scottish historian, who was later tutor to the young James VI, criticised the large amounts of money the king spent – on tournaments, on royal palaces, and on the royal navy. He viewed it as excessive, in particular that James commissioned the building of a ship which was too big for any Scottish port and which required a new berthing to be built.

He describes him as a wasteful, spendthrift, who, if he had not died when he did, would have brought the country into financial ruin.

But if one puts this into context – this was after all the era of the dour John Knox, where criticisms were quick in flowing and compliments were almost frowned upon, one can see this for what it is – a negative and unbalanced account by a historian who was not keen to give much credit to a recent monarch.

The chronicler Sir David Lindsay, who was 23 when James IV died, is less judgemental. He describes him as a great leader who did much to improve law and justice in the country and who made his mark in European history.

By the end of the sixteenth century there was agreement by many of the chroniclers that James had been an able ruler who was much loved by his people, but who at the end would not listen to advice, the result of which was his untimely death.

Looking back five hundred years on, it is these accounts which ring true. There is no doubt that he was a fascinating character who organised bizarre social experiments, and who had a keen desire to further his knowledge in science. He was certainly an active ruler, travelling all over Scotland, and playing an active part in improving law and justice throughout the country. He was well liked, and his people certainly seemed happy with him. Outside the Highlands and Islands there was little unrest during his rule. Norman McDougall, in his biography of him, written in the late twentieth century, writes that he was diplomatically naïve in going to war. Perhaps he was, but hindsight is a great thing, and we must remember both that he had a largely peaceful reign, and that war with England was often popular with the Scottish people.

The 2012 excavation of a body which was later confirmed to be that of King Richard III of England set many people thinking about where the body of the Scottish King James IV is. Following Flodden, James's body was embalmed at Berwick and placed in a lead coffin and sent to London. Katherine of Aragon, who was in charge of the country while her husband Henry fought in France, is said to have sent James's bloodstained and slashed surcoat to her husband, with the suggestion that he use it as a war banner.

James's body lay in the Carthusian Monastery of Sheen, seven miles from London, where it lay unburied for months while Henry awaited a reply from the pope as to what to do with the excommunicated king. On 29 November Leo replied that, as it was presumed that the king had repented his sins before he died, Henry could, as he wished, bury the Scottish king, with full funeral honours.

But the body wasn't buried. It is unknown why, but eventually it was forgotten about. We can find reference to it in a book published in 1575 titled *The Flower of Fame*, which states that, 'The dead body of the King of Scottes was found among the other carcasses in the fielde and from thence brought to London, and so through London streets on horseback. And from thence it was carried to Sheene (neere unto Brentford), whereat the Queen then lay, and there the perjured carcas lyeth unto this day unburied.'

The next mention we have of the king's body was in Elizabethan times when a master glazier is said to have taken the head home, until his wife got fed up of it and made him get rid of it. There are also accounts from that time of workmen at the monastery using the head to play football with.

Following this, the head was taken to Great St Michael's Church in Wood Street, which by the twentieth century was a pub called, ironically, 'The Red Herring'. Here it was dumped in a charnel pit. The Sheen Monastery where the rest of the body is thought to have been left, was demolished following the dissolution of the monasteries.

But while the whereabouts of James's skeleton is not known, we do know the location of his sword, dagger and the ring he was given by Queen Anne of France. Or do we?

As happens in battle the victors took what they could from the dead. Hence James's ring, sword and dagger were taken from his corpse to be given to the Earl of Surrey, soon to be the Earl of Norfolk. The relics would later be mentioned in *The Life, Correspondence and Collections of Thomas Howard, Earl of Arundel* published in 1921. Earl of Norfolk was another one of Arundel's titles.

The book states that tradition asserts that he killed James IV of Scotland 'with his own hand' and that the three items were sent by Henry, 6th Duke of Norfolk, in 1682 to be kept at the College of Arms in London. The book also contains a copy of the deed recording the loan of the sword, dagger and ring, making clear that future dukes would be allowed to take the relics back should they wish.

In 2009 Elspeth Crocket, a retired modern languages teacher from West Dunbartonshire, wrote to the current Duke of Norfolk to request that these items be returned to Scotland, to be displayed to the public, potentially at the Museum of Scotland or at the Palace of Holyrood House. The College of Arms, in their response, denied all knowledge of the proviso that subsequent dukes of Norfolk could, if they wished, request the return of these artefacts, and raised the issue that there were doubts on the authenticity of the items.

This was not the first request for the return of the relics. Writer David Ross and a group of people from museums in the Borders had made previous unsuccessful requests for the relics to be returned to Scotland, even temporarily.

Indeed, there have been questions surrounding the authenticity of the items. One expert, from the University of Glasgow, stated that the sword and dagger could be dated to the late sixteenth century, several years after Flodden. Other experts agree with him.

However, other experts, from both Scotland and Spain argue that they are confident that the weapons date from the time of James IV. It is particularly interesting to hear the point of view of Spanish experts as, according to Agnes Mure McKenzie's *The Rise of the Stewarts*, published in 1935, the weapons were presented to James by the Spanish ambassador. We should also take into account the fact that Spanish weapons at this time were advanced and perhaps resembled what would be found in other parts of Europe fifty to one hundred years later.

It has also been argued that, as it was normal in the past to replace and improve on objects to ensure they stayed up to date, it is feasible that these are the original items and that they were simply added to after Flodden.

By 2013, as the 500th anniversary approached, it looked as if progress was being made. Gary Stewart of the Society of William Wallace and Dr Elspeth King of the Smith Art Gallery were liaising with the College of Arms, negotiating the terms of a loan, in order for the artefacts to be returned to Scotland. The Stirling Smith museum would house the display from August until October.

Nationalist MSP Christine Grahame tabled a motion in the Scottish Parliament calling for this, which received cross party support. At last some progress was being made, and excitement was building. How amazing it would be to see the king's belongings returned to Scotland for the first time in 500 years.

But it was not to be. Loan costs of more than £10,000 were to prove prohibitive. The loan was cancelled and the artefacts remained in London.

Are the relics authentic? Will they ever be returned to Scotland? Will we ever locate his skeleton and skull? James IV was a fascinating and charismatic man when he was alive, so it should not surprise us that more than 500 years after his death he is keeping historians and archaeologists talking and debating. The case of Richard III gives us hope that progress may be made, and perhaps in time his remains, as well as his belongings, will be returned north to where they belong.

Bibliography

Accounts of the Lord High Treasurer of Scotland, 1473-1513

Bulletins of the history of medicine

Buchanan G, *History of Scotland, 1582*

Buchanan, G, *History of Scotland 2 Blackie, Fullerton and Co, 1827*

Buchanan Patricia, *Margaret Tudor,* 1985

Cherry A, *Princes, poets and patrons*, 1987 edition

Elliot, William F, *The Battle of Flodden and the raids of 1513,* 1991

Greene, Robert, *The Scottish history of James IV,* 1977

Leslie, John, *The History of Scotland, 1436-1561,* Edinburgh 1831

Lindsay, Robert of Pitscottie, *The Chronicles of Scotland, 1436-1604,* Edinburgh 1814

MacDougall, N, *James IV*, 1997

MacDougall, N, *James III,* 1982

Mackie, R, L, *King James IV of Scotland*, 1958

Mackie, *James IV, Letters of James the Fourth, edited by R.L.*

Mackie, *Scottish History Society*, 1953

Reese, Peter, *Flodden,* 2003

Smith, Gregory G, *The Days of James IV,* 1889

Short, A, J, *James IV of Scotland, Sovereign and Surgeon*, 1992

Taylor, Ida A, *The Life of James IV,* 1913

Index

Printed in Great Britain
by Amazon

12487121R00068